DEMOCRATIC TYRANNY
AND
THE ISLAMIC PARADIGM

Democratic Tyranny *and* The Islamic Paradigm

AISHA
ABDURRAHMAN
BEWLEY

DIWAN ✦ PRESS

Classical and Contemporary Books on Islam and Sufism

Democratic Tyranny and the Islam Paradigm

Published by: Diwan Press Ltd.
311 Allerton Road
Bradford
BD15 7HA
UK

Website: www.diwanpress.com
email: info@diwanpress.com

By: Aisha Bewley

A catalogue record of this book is available from the British Library.

ISBN-13:   978-1-908892-48-5 (paperback)
                    978-1-908892-65-2 (ePub & Kindle)
Printed and bound by: Lightning Source

Contents

Preface (2025)

Having been requested to compose a short preface to the French translation of the text, I realised that it gave me an opportunity to address the current state of politics and the rather dire situation in which democracy now finds itself. We are living in a time of upheaval, a time of inflection, after which things could go in a number of directions, some extremely unpalatable. Democracy does now strikingly appear to be in retreat, a fact recognised even by those at the top of politics. The current American Vice-President, J.D. Vance, stated categorically in an interview that the current order will meet its 'inevitable collapse'. Peter Thiel, the billionaire venture capitalist and political activist, has said that he does not believe that liberty and democracy are compatible. The list of critics of democracy today goes on and on. A large number of people have finally realised that democracy as practised leads to a tyranny controlled by an oligarchy. Its critics are growing. Its stalwart defendants tend to be part of what Curtis Yarvin has termed 'the Cathedral' – the interconnected bureaucratic network of academics, media elites and government bureaucrats who set the bounds of acceptable opinion and police it. The bureaucratic element of this situation is sometimes referred to as 'the Deep State', the Swamp, or the Blob. The natural response to this is expressed in the desire to dismantle this edifice or to 'drain the swamp'. Then the question arises: what political structure should then replace 'democracy'?

There are a number of alternative possibilities currently being put forward. Most prominent, of course, is the swing to the right in the form of populist nationalist authoritarianism, including a hankering for some form of 'monarchy' or rule by a single all-powerful leader. This seems to be common to all the alternatives currently being presented.

One possibility offered, and considered by some, owing to the power of Big Tech companies, to be already in operation, is techno-feudalism under the leadership of a techno-oligarchy with an all-powerful CEO, resembling a capitalist company. Curtis Marvin, the blogger formerly known as Mencius Moldbug, and Nick Land, the philosopher behind the 'Dark Enlightenment' and Neoreaction, advocate an accountable 'techno-monarchy' structured on the model of a start-up company. However, this is unworkable when faced with the reality of a large complex system. Therefore others propose a multitude of city-states under technocratic CEOs and look fondly at Singapore, Dubai and Hong Kong, although the latter did not work out so well.

Yaneer Bar-Yam, a specialist in complex systems, asks the question: 'Why should governments fail?'and then gives the answer:

Because leaders, whether self appointed dictators, or elected officials, are unable to identify what policies will be good for a complex society. The unintended consequences are beyond their comprehension. Regardless of values or objectives, the outcomes are far from what they intend. (Teams: A manifesto, New England Complex Systems Institute (July 31, 2016))

There is also the solution posed by the entrepreneur Balaji Srinivasan of Network States which develop from an online community. It is an interesting solution, but can a state exist without physical territory or actual real (non-digital) currency? Is it possible to re-engineer money into cryptocurrency alone when, by its nature, it is highly speculative?

'Neoliberalism' refers to the political-social set of beliefs and assumptions which has held sway since the 1970s. Vesting power in the markets, it empowers those with capital – the investors and entrepreneurs – and disempowers those who are employed, under the specious banners of democracy and equality (which lack any substantive meaning). Neoliberalism is really a construct of impulses used to maintain market and intellectual dominance with minimal government interference, presenting a facade of morality while actually obscuring its underlying racialism and its belief in the superiority of Western civilisation. It is, in fact, only the successful oligarchy who are the beneficiaries of the system.

Global neoliberalism appears to be coming to an end. Most trace the beginning of its demise to the 2008 financial crisis. There were other things also happening at the time which paved the way for that crisis - like Putin's first aggression against Georgia, the breakdown of the WTO and unproductive climate talks. Of course, all this did not come out of the blue. The disintegration of the gold standard in 1971 ultimately led to the unrestrained financial dealings which led to the crash of 2008. In addition, the psychological and financial impact of Covid exacerbated what Hannah Arendt points out as the problem of loneliness, which is a seedbed for totalitarianism, because it fosters an angry, aggrieved desire to escape the current situation. The term she uses is *Verlassenheit*, which means a state of being abandoned and hence left alone and alienated which accurately describes what the current system does to individuals.

In spite of the marketing assertion that a market untrammelled by government intervention would lead to optimum well-being, neoliberalism has, in fact, given rise to incredible inequality. The latest World Inequality Report shows that the richest 10% of people in the world own 76% of all wealth, while the poorest 50% have virtually none at all and many have negative wealth or debt. This stark disparity inevitably leads to isolation, despair and anger. 'Democracy' clearly is not working for the majority of the human race.

Most of the 'alternatives' to the current political system have been devised by people with some connection to Silicon Valley. Why then are the techno-oligarchy so unhappy with the prevailing status quo? Obviously the system has given them vast wealth and clout - just look at their prominent positions at the inauguration of Donald Trump. Yanis Varoufakis aptly designates them as the barons of techno-feudalism, based on their control of cloud capital. In fact, going back to 2008, they were helped by the central banks' reaction to the crisis which resulted in the handing out large quantities of money to them while most people were enduring austerity. Notably, nine of ten dollars spent by Facebook (now Meta) on cloud capital came from the money gifted to them by the central banks. That was where the money that was meant to go to households and small businesses ended up. Therefore the human cogs that physically make the system run are, justifiably, unhappy and angry.

But what do the new techno-oligarchs want? They offer no viable solutions to the current situation in the form of policy or helping those who are alienated or addressing the heart of the problem. Their answer is to simply eliminate any government interference and unleash unrestrained capitalism, forgetting that the original problem was brought about by precisely the same methodology. Or, cynically, perhaps with full awareness of it. So, in fact, the demise of neoliberalism is not what is actually taking place: it has even been referred to as the 'strange non-death of neoliberalism' (Colin Crouch). What is really being advocated is the jettisoning of any social responsibility for those in need and the removal of any state control over their interests. It is not surprising that the proponents of the 'Dark Enlightenment' are enamoured of the Middle Ages which was truly feudal with proper lords and serfs.

Thus the neo-right are also part of the project of neoliberalism. None of this constitutes post-neoliberalism, but is rather simply a mutation of neoliberalism, since the goal of neoliberalism is the empowerment of the entrepreneurs and untrammelled freedom of markets. This is, as the historian Quinn Slobodian says, 'a bastard neo-liberal strain of crack-up capitalism.' The populist nationalists remain neoliberals in respect of the market, but with a xenophobic solution which posits that removing 'others' will solve the problem they face. They do occasionally take pot shots at certain aspects of the neoliberal structure, but it is largely out of yearning for a return to a fabled golden past. Steve Bannon and his fellow travellers - of whom numerous examples are found in political parties in Europe - are traditionalists: they want to go back to a golden past by destroying the corrupt present. This requires an authoritarian leader, so at least they agree with the techno-feudalists on this point. And it further entails the dissolution of large state bureaucracies and inter-national institutions like the U.N. and the European Union, and international trade blocs. All of this noise is nevertheless useless against the insuperable capitalist imperative.

The nation-state is a paradigm that has only existed since the Treaty of Westphalia in 1648 which ended the Thirty Years' War. It paved the way for the separation of religion and state and legitimised usury (a consequence of Calvin's hermeneutical interpretation of Scripture). Neoliberalism has moved political power from the nation-state to the markets and now views the interference of national governance to be a hindrance to the capitalist project. This is where we find ourselves today and it is clear that no one is happy with the status quo - not even the obscenely rich. None of the solutions offered by the political movements outlined in this discussion address the underlying cause which has ultimately created the situation in which we now find ourselves. Bannon, for instance, believes in capitalism, but in a 'Judeo-Christian capitalism', which fails to acknowledge the pernicious root problem: the unjust usurious world economic system which enables the excessive accumulation of wealth in the hands of a few.

If one abandons the nation-state, there are two possible directions to take. One is centripetal, resulting in a return to empires, but the isolation engendered by the modern world works against that. The other direction is centrifugal, meaning the creation of smaller political entities. We see this in the proposal of smaller city-states or network states.

Instead of attempting to revive a romanticised Gilded Age, forgetting (or perhaps not) all the inequalities and injustices that took place in it, real alternatives need to be considered, which is why I believe we should put the model of Islamic governance on the table. I do not mean the Islamist model which arises when someone picks up a copy of *Islam for Dummies* and then adds their own misogynist, authoritarian, violent, or fantasist view and ends up with something that in no way resembles any past society based on Islamic principles. Nor does it mean trying to bring back the past. A principle of Islamic jurisprudence is *'urf,* or the normative practice of the people. For instance, in the past in the Middle East, a man was not considered to have judicial integrity if he did not wear a head covering, be it a turban, fez, or whatever. This did not, however, apply in western North Africa because that was not the custom, or *'urf* there. *'Urf* allows for customs that are in common practice to be applied in law as long as the custom does not go against an explicit text. This allows for flexibility and adaptability.

In the Islamic paradigm, the function of the ruler is to protect the weak against the strong, and part of that is to prevent the disproportionate accumulation of wealth in the hands of a few at the expense of the poor and to remove corruption from the courts of justice and other domains. In the Qur'an prayer is coupled with *zakat*. The market is not a sphere of interest which is independent of morality. If you do not solve the problem of usury, from which capitalism and neoliberalism spring, you cannot solve the social and political problems prevalent in today's world. It is only the Islamic paradigm that makes this imperative paramount.

In the Islamic paradigm there exists a ruler, but one who represents his people and has to tend to them and their well-being like a shepherd. The Prophet said, 'Everyone of you is a shepherd, and everyone of you is responsible for his flock; the caliph who rules the people is a shepherd, and he is responsible for those whom he governs.' If you read Shaykh Uthman dan Fodio's description of the ruler, it is evident that this role is very different to that of a CEO of a capitalist company. While network state has potential, its digital nature and lack of physical presence in both territory and currency is in danger of turning it into a LARP (Life Action Role Play) project. Nevertheless, that model could potentially facilitate connections between smaller communities.

More importantly, the Islamic paradigm is more than just a political project, because the principal function of governance is to enable the Muslims to fulfil their obligations both to Allah and to the other people in society. This negates the *Verlassenheit* or loneliness/isolation which Arendt posited as a seedbed for totalitarianism and for all the mutant forms of decayed neoliberalism prevalent today. This objective must never be forgotten. If it is, what happens will turn into a project disconnected from the worship of Allah and the establishment of social justice, and one that will almost certainly lead to people falling into the same traps that have ensnared all those others we have mentioned who are now seeking for something beyond 'democracy'.

'Democratic' Tyranny

THE MODERN 'democratic' world lives under the delusion that the much-vaunted democratic liberal political institutions of the West, the so-called 'civilised' world, somehow provide a guarantee of man's freedom and that this is the only natural and just form of governance possible. Indeed, in the modern world, so pervasive is this assumption, that it seems almost impossible to conceive of any other 'reasonable' form of governance.

Although people are very free in their use of the word 'democracy', it is very rare that anyone actually knows what 'democracy' really is. 'Human rights', 'liberty', 'equality' and 'democracy' have become emotive slogans that are parroted without any thought for what they actually mean – 'by the people, of the people, for the people.' What does it mean? What is this democratic ideal? Their actual meaning and their origins and consequences are largely ignored and indeed forgotten. They are slogans lacking in any real content.

Certainly the democracy bandied about today has nothing to do with its generally supposed origin, the democracy of the ancient Athenians, which was a very different concept indeed, nor is it based on a spiritual equality derived from a theoretical concept of universal Christian brotherhood which would envisage all its members as spiritual brothers who are all equal on the basis of their faith. If democracy did not come from the Greeks nor from the European Judaeo-Christian tradition, then where did it come from?

It will be shown that modern 'democracy' is actually the child of liberal individualism, which in turn rose from the ruins of the Universal Church after Luther, Calvin and Henry VIII succeeded in demolishing it. It will be seen that the Reformation, and Calvin in particular, were not only answerable for two things: the legalisation of usury and the opening of the gates to the accumulation of wealth on a previously unprecedented scale, but also for providing the model for the foundations of the modern nation-state. It was Geneva, not France, which gave birth to Rousseau. Artificial credit growth and 'democracy' are all too often to be found going hand-in-hand.

This poses many questions about the true nature of the modern political system and its relationship with the underlying economic structure. To obtain an understanding of this system that has become all pervasive, we must go back to the beginnings of Western political theory.

The Plato Scenario

IRST WE MUST examine the political origins of the West in the ancient world. When the ideas of republicanism and democracy began to be bandied about after the Renaissance and Enlightenment, the classical models were thought of as the ancient models of just government. But what did the Greeks really think? What was this original democracy?

For the ancient Greeks, governance fell basically into three fundamental categories – democracy, monarchy and oligarchy[1] and these were much discussed and debated. Although Athens was the propagator of democracy, almost all the Greek thinkers who have come down to us rejected democracy as an inferior form of government – no doubt based on empirical experience, and thought of monarchy as an intermediate form. This, of course, is not hereditary monarchy, but the rule of a single leader.

At its pinnacle in the time of Pericles, offices in Athens were filled by lots and the officials were directed by the decisions taken by the Assembly which included, in principle, every Athenian citizen (excluding women, slaves and foreigners). Every citizen had *isegoria*, the right to express himself regarding a decision before that decision was taken or before a war was embarked on. They would never have called modern 'democracy' democracy. They would have called it 'elective oligarchy'. When was the last time a modern electorate was asked if it wanted to go to war? Furthermore, in the course of his lifetime, every citizen would inevitably participate in the administrative branch of the government at some point. But 'democracy' was by no means beneficial or benevolent towards those unfortunate enough not to be Athenians, and to be at the receiving end of this 'democracy' was not at all pleasant (as in the case of Melos.[2])

In *The History of the Peloponnesian War*, we find Thucydides describing the destruction of a political system that might well be described as Athenian enlightened self-interest. His thesis is that an individualist and democratic order releases great energy which, when directed by sound leadership as in the case of Pericles, provides security, prestige and economic gain.[3] However, the system is fundamentally unstable and will be ultimately destroyed. Thucydides much admired the more closed oligarchic structure of Sparta for its stability. He describes what happened to Athens after Pericles[4]:

> Pericles, by his rank, ability and known integrity, was able to exercise an independent control over the masses – to lead them instead of being led by them; for as he never sought power by improper means, he was never compelled to flatter them...what was nominally a democracy became in his hands government by the first citizen. With his successors it was different. More on a level with one another, and each grasping at supremacy, they ended by committing even the conduct of state affairs to the whims of the multitude. This, as might have been expected in a great imperial state, produced a host of blunders. (II, 66)

Herodotus in particular pointed out that the goal of governance is stability and justice, while democracy, through its encouragement of rival cliques and its susceptibility to demagoguery, ends up as tyrannical rule. Or, on the other hand, corruption and malpractice can lead to mutually supporting cliques until the 'people's champion' arises and soon assumes absolute authority. One thing is noticeable – and that is the innate intolerance of democracy to other forms of governance – a tendency much in evidence today. Those who deviated from the norm tended to find themselves condemned to ostracism or even death – Socrates, Anaxagoras, Protagoras. You were free to express yourself, but could find yourself in trouble if you said the wrong thing or had the wrong friends.

For these men who criticised democracy, they thought that the best ruler was the monarch or single ruler who respected the natural laws which were, in the end, God-given.[5] Indeed, Athens functioned most efficiently under Pericles who was a strong and stable leader with great respect for the laws.

Aristotle is no less critical of democracy, considering it to be wrong and degenerate, and mentions demagogues as the greatest peril:

> Demagogues arise in states where the laws are not sovereign. The people then become an autocrat – a simple composite autocrat made up of many members, with the many playing the sovereign, not as individuals...A democracy of this order, being in the nature of an autocrat and not being governed by law, begins to attempt an autocracy. It grows despotic; flatterers come to be held in honour; it becomes analogous to the tyrannical form of single-person government. (*Politics*, IV, iv, 26-28)[6]

The ultimate political analysis is found in Plato's *Republic*[7] where he analyzes all types of power and the movement to democracy which goes hand-in-hand with the decline of human society, from timocracy to oligarchy to democracy and ultimately to tyranny. Oligarchy develops from timocracy when wealth flows into the stores of certain individuals. His description of the effects of a wealth-oriented oligarchy is as apt today as it was then:

'...In an oligarchy, then, this neglect to curb riotous living sometimes reduces to poverty men of a not ungenerous nature. They settle down in idleness, some of them burdened with debt, some disfranchised, some both at once; and these drones are armed and can sting. Hating the men who have acquired their property and conspiring against them and the rest of society, they long for a revolution. Meanwhile the usurers, intent upon their own business, seem unaware of their existence; they are too busy planting their own stings into any fresh victim who offers them an opening to inject the poison of their money; and while they multiply their capital by usury, they are also multiplying the drones and paupers. When the danger threatens to break out, they will do nothing to quench the flames, either in the way we mentioned, by forbidding a man to do what he likes with his own, or by the next best remedy, which would be a law enforcing a respect for right conduct. If it were enacted that, in general, voluntary contracts for a loan should be made at the lender's risk, there would be less of this shameless pursuit of wealth and a scantier crop of those evils I have just described.' (*Republic*, Chap 31.)

It is love of wealth and the stress on the honour derived from increasing it that causes virtue to be neglected and despised. In the oligarchy, the rulers are rich and everyone else is poor. Then the oligarchs seek to become richer still through usury while they neglect the education of the young, allowing them to become licentious and idle. So when the rulers become weak, the poor rise up and overthrow them – either with foreign help or through factions among the oligarchs. This democracy is, as he says, 'full of all freedom of action, and of speech, and of liberty, to do in it what any one inclines.' Thus a person's appetites are many and varied. He follows one at one moment and another at another moment. As wealth was the slogan of oligarchy, so 'liberty' is the slogan of democracy. Plato gives a brilliant description of life in a democracy when he describes the democratic young man:

Knowledge, right principles, true thoughts, are not at their post; and the place lies open to the assault of false and presumptuous notions... Modesty and self-control, dishonoured and insulted as the weaknesses of an unmanly fool, are thrust out into exile; and the whole crew of unprofitable desires take a hand in banishing moderation and frugality, which, as they will have it, are nothing but churlish meanness. So they take possession of the soul which they have swept clean, as if purified for initiation into higher mysteries; and nothing remains but to marshal the great procession bringing home Insolence, Anarchy, Waste and Impudence, whose resplendent divinities are crowned with garlands, whose praises they sing under flattering names: Insolence, they call good breeding, Anarchy freedom, Waste magnificence, and Impudence a manly spirit.

... He declares that one appetite is as good as another and all must have their equal rights. So he spends his days indulging the pleasure of the moment, now intoxicated with wine and music, and then taking to a spare diet and drinking nothing but water; one day in hard training, the next doing nothing at all, the third apparently immersed in study. Every now and then he takes a part in politics, leaping to his feet to say whatever comes into his head... His life is subject to no order or restraint, and he has no wish to change an existence which he calls pleasant, free, and happy.

Then matters proceed to the next stage. Plato says, 'out

of no other republic is tyranny constituted but out of democracy, out of the most excessive liberty I imagine comes the greatest and most savage tyranny.' Eventually an adventurer and a demagogue, usually with military background, calls himself 'the friend of the people' and sets himself up as president or prime minister. Then he needs a bodyguard to protect him, thus establishing his power. Thus unrestrained liberty results in unrestrained servitude.

Certainly the description of the character of the people which ultimately leads to the despotic state is much like the situation today:

> Law-abiding citizens will be insulted as nonentities who hug their chains; and all praise and honour will be bestowed on rulers who behave like subjects and subjects who behave like rulers... The parent falls into the habit of behaving like the child, and the child like the parent; the father is afraid of his sons, and they show no fear or respect for their parents, in order to assert their freedom. Citizens, resident aliens, and strangers from abroad are all on an equal footing. To descend to smaller matters, the schoolmaster timidly flatters his pupils, and the pupils make light of their masters as well as of their attendants. Generally speaking, the young copy their elders, argue with them, and will not do as they are told; while the old, anxious not to be thought disagreeable tyrants, imitate the young and condescend to enter into their jokes and amusements.

The outcome of all this excessive freedom can only be excessive subjection. The despot has not a friend in the world he can trust because he is under the dominance of his desires. He is the most miserable of men, full of fears and desires, never satisfied, never secure.

In the end of *The Republic* Plato concludes that the

polity must have governance and that the best ruler is the philosopher-king rather than the *demos* (the people), an ideal which may well be unobtainable in this world, but is nonetheless true. In *The Laws*, he states that in the absence of a moral ruler who can react to situations and implement the laws in the best possible manner, the code of laws is the best instrument of government and the rulers are the 'guardians of the laws'. No one has yet equalled Plato's succinct description of political forms and how they reflect the moral state of man.

Another point that must be noted is the Athenian double standard, for while Athens was a democracy at **home**, it was an empire abroad in relation to the rest of the known world. As Thucydides quotes Pericles in a speech:

> Again, your country has a right to your services in sustaining the glories of her position. These are a common source of pride to you all, and you cannot decline the burdens of empire and still expect to share its honours. The issue is not only slavery or independence, but also loss of empire and danger from the animosities to which it has exposed you. Besides, to recede is no longer possible, if indeed any of you in the alarm of the moment has become enamoured of the honesty of such an unambitious part. What you hold is, to speak frankly, a despotism; perhaps it was wrong to take it, but to let it go is unsafe. (ii, 63)

He goes on:

> If we should be forced to yield, still it will be remembered that we held rule over more Greeks than any other Greek state, that we sustained the greatest wars against their united or separate powers, and inhabited a city unrivalled by any other in resources or

magnitude. These glories may incur the censure of the slow and unambitious; but in the breast of energy they will awake emulation...' (ii, 64)

This was an economic as well as political imperialism. Some time in the early 440's, the Athenians passed a decree prescribing the use of Athenian currency, weights and measures throughout the Confederacy. The decree even went so far as to say: 'If anyone proposes or votes in this matter that it is legitimate to use foreign coinage or to make a loan therein he is to be reported to the Eleven without delay. The Eleven shall pass sentence of death.' Hardly a libertarian measure!

Notes

1. Plato has four, including timocracy, a form of government dominated by ambition, as in Sparta, and Aristotle gives two types of each: kingship, aristocracy, polity, tyranny, oligarchy and democracy.

2. The island of Melos was conquered by Athens in 416 BC because they refused to pay tribute – whereupon all men of military age were killed and the rest of the populace imprisoned. Thucydides describes a meeting between the Athenians and the Melians in which the Athenians state that it is natural that 'the stronger should rule the weaker', i.e. democracy was only for the Athenians.

3. Mind you, Socrates was not averse to pointing out that these 'great leaders' failed abysmally to elevate those under them: 'You praise the men who feasted the citizens and satisfied their desires and people say that they have made the city great, not seeing that the swollen and ulcerated conditions of the State is to be attributed to these elder statesmen, for they have filled the city full of harbours, docks and walls and left no room for justice and temperance.' (Gorgias)

4. Of course, at the end of his life, the Athenians convicted Pericles of theft and nearly executed him.

5. The question of the Greek view of the God-given nature of the laws would require a lengthy discussion. In Homer, the King's judgement of laws are called *themistes*, as originating from Themis, the embodiment of divine authority. This is reinforced by *dike*, justice which became embodied in a goddess in Hesiod. Originally *dike* was the declaration of that which is *themis*, so the two are connected. *Nomos* is more secular,

like custom or conventional usage.

6. This is like what Edmond About said about the French democrat who 'looks with pride at his face in the glass as he shaves in the morning, remembering that he is the forty-millionth part of a tyrant, and forgetting that he is the whole of a slave.'

7. The word for 'Republic' is *politeia* or polity, which really means a political constitution in general.

The Republic should not be taken as Plato's vision of an attainable state – it is an extreme illustration of the ultimate consequences of certain political principles when put into practice. A more attainable and pragmatic model of governance is found in *The Laws*.

The Humanist Republic

HISTORICALLY, the arena of political development then moves to Rome. Roman law is the basis of all European jurisprudence and it is Rome that gave us what we would call the idea of 'authority' – not power, which derives from the human ability to act in concert, but authority, which refers to how you are governed in a political context, for effective governance without authority is impossible. Aptly expressed in Cicero's famous axiom, *Quum potestas in populo, auctoritas in Senatu sit* ('Power lies with the people, authority in the Senate'), authority was originally thought to be that which requires neither coercion nor persuasion, but rather commands respect. The need for authority was taken for granted – it was a question of who should exercise it, under what conditions and what limits.

Cicero said that the law of nature is the constitution of the world and is universal and eternal[1] and its aim is to promote the common good and to achieve justice. This is a shift in viewpoint from that of the Greeks. There is not the same respect for the *nomos* (law) which means an old formulation of law which has a social aspect and so is custom as well as law.[2] It is not specific like the statutory *lex* nor is it nature which is seen as unordered. The *nomoi* do, nonetheless, also have a divine origin, being a gift of the gods, represent wise opinion and the basis of political association.

The consequence of this shift is that the allegiance which the citizen owes to the laws of his particular state is conditional and not absolute, for if they do not conform to the laws of nature, he is under no moral obligation to obey them. Plato thought that the philosopher – who is so rare as to be virtually non-existent – had this discrimination, but Cicero thought that every man has the capacity. This further entails the doctrine of the natural equality of men.[3] He goes on to say that that which makes people fellow-citizens is their allegiance to the same law. This is not the same as being 'by nature' a member of a state. They are fellow citizens by virtue of accepting the same Law and by thus choosing to be part of this commonwealth.

Rome gave us the idea of the state, and the distinction between state and society (Cicero, *De Re Publica*).[4] Although 'republic' is derived from the original *res publica*, it would more accurate to translate it as 'commonwealth'. Rome also developed the concept of legal and moral 'rights'. It was the *lex regia* which gave the Emperor authority. So when Octavius became the Emperor Augustus, he did so as the *princeps* of the Senate, the 'first citizen', in other words he simply extended the natural authority which already existed, rather than seeming to usurp it. As the *princeps* became the monarch, this seemed, on the whole, to be a natural extension of the original position. He still represented the people, and his power was based on delegation, not personal right.

When the Roman form was recast in Christian form, it relegated all authority to God who in turn conferred it on the rulers, which came ultimately to be known as 'divine right', referring to the institution of rule rather than the individual ruler.

This came about by the Christian Church looking at things through the Roman legal mode of thinking – reinforced by the Vulgate, or Latin translation of the Hebrew and Greek Bible by St Jerome. The Latin language which he used reflected that of the Roman jurists and thus the whole view of the Bible was imbued with Roman legal tones – not necessarily in harmony with the original Greek or Hebrew.

Thus in Latin Christianity, the relations between God and man came to be viewed as legal relations, conceived in a Roman framework of rights and duties.[5]

Of course, the Emperor was not keen to be relegated to a secondary role. He also adopted Biblical support for his (pre-Christian) position – the Emperor is the 'Living Law' – He is the Autokrator,[6] who represents the Pantokrator (God). Imperial laws were 'sacred laws' and his pronouncements 'divine'. Actually, what we have is the pagan idea of the divine Roman emperor as the 'Lord of the world' reappearing in Christian garb. This led to the intermittent conflict between the Pope and Emperor. One saw the Christian Roman Church and the other the Roman Christian Church.

According to the Gelasian thesis based on Pauline doctrine,[7] stressing the split of the pope's *auctoritas* and the emperor's *regis potestas*,[8] the Pope is the head and temporal rulership is a direct gift.[9] The emperor is hence an auxiliary with no autonomous character. The later dissemination of this view, of course, had inevitable political consequences. It severed the relation between the ruler and his people. Based on the Pauline idea of power passing straight from God, the people had not conferred power on the ruler and so they could not take it away. The ruler had no intrinsic right to rule and the people had no intrinsic rights to demand anything from the ruler.[10]

Furthermore, the codification of Roman law in the Code of Justinian (*Corpus Juris Civilis*) which took place between 427 and 533 had a crucial effect on the medieval approach to governance. Needless to say, it conveyed Roman ideology and culture, and became the model for most of the Middle Ages. Justinian's position was that it was the monarch who was the ultimate sovereign ruler.

The conflict between the two views led to the dualist theory of the separation of Church and state (*sacerdotium* and *regnum*) by the twelfth century. It was first advanced by the German Henry IV in the Investiture Contest, who viewed the Church's claim to monarchic sovereignty as a usurpation. Needless to say, Henry's arguments had no effect at all on the Pope who promptly deposed him.[11] The only way to move from the theocratic argument where the ruler stands above the law and is not subject to any checks, or descending authority, is through revolution.[12]

Thomas Aquinas (d. 1274), for all his scholastic problems and failure to grasp the consequences of legal devices which allowed usury,[13] resuscitated the Greek (Aristotelian in his case) and Roman concept that the polity (*civitas*) was a natural congregation of men. A man could be a 'citizen' without being a Christian,[14] other states were also legitimate since they were natural, and he defined the political (or ascending) government (*regimen politicum*) as opposed to the descending or theocratic government (*regimen regale*). Although he himself preferred a combination of the two, he opened the way to attack both the papacy and the very idea of theocratic governance. Although he recognised that all men were equal in the sight of God, he still maintained the hierarchical view, perhaps not surprising in view of his devotion to Aristotle.

The first major step on the way to the modern scenario of democracy then moves to the Italian City Republics. The earliest city to adopt consular governance rather than hereditary monarchy was Pisa in 1085, and then it spread rapidly through Lombardy and Tuscany in the next fifty years. The consuls were changed regularly at first and then the consuls were superseded by an elective government centred on the *podestà*, who had supreme power (*potestas*) over the city. He was usually a citizen of another city to ensure his impartiality. He was elected and ruled with two main councils, a larger one and an inner or secret council of about forty important citizens. He was a salaried official and could not initiate political decisions. This Republican self-government became widespread throughout Northern Italy by the twelfth century. Even though they were *de facto* independent, *de iure* they were vassals of the Holy Roman Empire. They resisted all attempts to reimpose the rule of the Emperor over them, proclaiming their 'liberty', i.e. independence and self-government.

None of this had any legal basis. As already stated, the law studied at the time had been based on the Roman civil code, and those who studied this code, the Glossators, were quite literal in the application of Justinian's Code. Thus the Emperor was still technically the *princeps* of Justinian and the sole ruler of all (*dominus mundi*). The idea of an independent minor rule or the people as an identity having authority carried no weight at all in this view. When the Roncaglian Decrees of Frederick Barbarossa were drawn up in 1158, they even denied the cities the right to appoint their own *podestà*.[15]

Then something crucial to political thought took place in the fourteenth century. This change of perspective occurred in the school of the Post-Glossators, founded by Bartolus of Saxoferrato (1314 – 52). He said that where facts and law are in conflict, the law must be changed to fit the facts, and not the reverse, pointing out that while the Emperor *de iure* had claim to be the sole ruler, many people *de facto* did not obey him. He ends by basically saying that the Emperor must accept facts. He develops his argument to the point where he says the free Italian cities – and hence eventually kingdoms – were a *sibi princeps*, a *princeps* unto themselves, i.e. implicitly they are independent states. The people could make their laws and authority stemmed from them. This is the first move to the modern legal concept of the state. In the Bartolist view, the people elected their Council and it represented them. The people themselves were the source of authority.

With this potential power vacuum created by the rejection of the power of the Emperor, the Papacy stepped in to re-assert its claim to temporal as well as spiritual power. This position of the Pope being a temporal power especially dates from Innocent IV in the twelfth century and Boniface VIII. This led the Lombards and Tuscans to counter that the power of the Empire was separate from the Church. This left them in an unenviable position – trying to defend themselves from the Empire on one hand and the Church on the other. Professing the authority of either one would lose them their independence.

The response to this was formulated by Marsiglio of Padua[16] (c. 1275-1342) in his *Defensor Pacis* (*The Defender of Peace*), a controversial discourse which forced him to flee for live to Bavaria. Whereas Bartolus' theory was legal and aimed at the relation of small kingdoms to the Emperor, Marsiglio also took on the Church and flatly stated that the Church had no claim to spiritual authority:

'Not only did Christ himself refuse rulership or coercive judgement in this world, whereby he furnished an example for his apostles and disciples and their successors to do likewise, but also he taught by words and showed by example that all men, both priests and non-priests, should be subject in property and in person to the coercive judgement of the rulers of this world.' (Discourse II, IV, 9)

He goes on to say that the Legislator of each independent kingdom is the sole possessor of 'coercive jurisdiction' over every person, no matter what his status. Good government rests on popular sovereignty and the king is elected by the people and responsible to them and bound by laws. Bartolus also said that the citizens of a city 'constitute their own *princeps*' and that the 'right of judgement' of rulers is delegated to them (*concessum est*) by the people. A rationalist to the core, who most likely would have been more at home in the Enlightenment, Marsiglio stated that there was no evidence that God had instituted human government. Life in the Hereafter might well be important, but it was of little concern here where the goal was 'good living'. Little wonder that to be a Marsilian was as subversive as the term Marxist was later. He and his assistant, John of Jandun, were declared heretics as well as 'the sons of the devil' and 'pestiferous men'.

The view of popular sovereignty of Marsiglio and Bartolus was a radical springboard. Sovereignty lies with the people who can only delegate and never alienate it. No legitimate ruler is ever more than an official appointed by – and liable to dismissal by – the people. This was in reference to a city, a *civitas*, but, of course, it is a logical progression to apply it to a *regnum*. This, at the time, was completely at variance with the traditional Medieval, and indeed the Thomist view of a necessary monarch to prevent factions.

The classical pattern of democracy descending into chaos and ultimately into tyrannt as described by Plato took place in the Italian cities. The power of patriciate oligarchies was taken over by some democratic forms, as in Geneva where the *Rat* (aristocratic Council) was replaced in 1337. An even stronger parallel is seen in the instances where the newly enriched merchant class determined to cease power. These *popolani* would often then exile the older nobility. This led to constant feuding and battles between the factions. By the end of the thirteenth century, internal factions and the resulting chaos led to the suspensions of constitutions and to the rule of a strong *signore* or despot, starting with Ferrara where the Etensi family became the permanent rulers. In Verona, it was the leader of the *popolani*, the *Capitano del Popolo*, who founded the ruling dynasty.

Ure examines the development of the despots in Italy in his *Origin of Tyranny* and equates seventh and sixth century Greek tyrants with the Italian tyranny of the Renaissance, stressing the role of usury. As regards the Greeks, he says that their tyrants 'were the first men in their various cities to realise the political possibilities of new conditions created by the introduction of a new coinage, and that to a large extent they owed their position as tyrants to a financial or commercial supremacy which they had already established.' He goes to compare them to the system built up 'by the rich bankers and merchants who made themselves despots in so many of the city states of Italy. The most famous of these are the Medici, the family who gave a new power to the currency by their development of the banking business... and became tyrants of Florence... Another despot at Bologna was the rich usurer Romeo Pepoli.'[17] He mentions the various rich merchants who took power.[18]

There was a hankering in Florence by most Florentines, like Dante, for a strong autocratic government ruled by a monarch. In the much debated view of Hans Baron[19], views altered due to the crisis period of 1400-1402 when Florence was faced with absorption into Milan by the conquering Gian Galeazzo Visconti. Florence was saved by his sudden death, but the danger awakened them to their republican heritage. It was at this point that the humanists, like Leonardo Bruni, began to praise liberty and the Roman Republic – seeing Brutus as their hero rather than Caesar. In the *Livres dou Tresor*, Brunetto Latini (c. 1220-94), the chancellor of Florence's first popular government, mentions three types of governance – kings, aristocracies and peoples, and says that that of the peoples is by far the best.

Bruni, in his *Oration*, goes so far as to state that popular government is the only legitimate form of governance because it 'makes possible true liberty and equality before the law for the whole body of citizens' and 'enables the virtues to flourish.' (p. 3) He also stresses the equality of the citizens who must all have equal opportunity to serve the community to the highest level they can achieve.

According to Baron, there are two new characteristics here, while others consider them to be a continuing development: the assumption that historical development is due to natural causes and the sense that a particular political community is a continuing entity whose existence is not dependent on the men and government of any given time. As fact is often not in accord with reality, it is interesting to note that Bruni, who had been Chancellor of the republic of Florence, spent his latter years during Medici domination quietly reading Plato instead of continuing to praise republican freedom.

Another aspect of the humanist picture is the revival of a version of classical *virtus* (virtue) praised by Petrarch. Cicero was his gate to the *vir virtutis* and the quest for universal excellence. This required the jettisoning of the Augustinian picture of man. In the *City of God*, Augustine stated that the pursuit of *virtus* was based on an arrogant and erroneous view of what man was capable of obtaining by his own efforts. If a ruler governs virtuously, that is only due to the grace of God, not his own efforts, and in any case, man can never be perfect because he is fundamentally corrupt. The traditional Medieval Christian position was that man was incapable of such excellence. (see Innocent III, *On the Misery of Man*)

Petrarch, on the other, says that men must obtain the cardinal virtues of antiquity (wisdom, fortitude, temperance, justice), and Christian faith as well. So there must be no arrogance in these virtues because their acquisition is due to God and must be informed by a constant desire to please God. Although they put *virtù* in a Christian context, all their heroes were pre-Christian! The abandonment of the sense of man as fundamentally corrupt and incapable was left further and further behind until the point was reached by someone like Giannozzo Manetti where he proclaims man's 'unmeasurable dignity and excellence' and the 'extraordinary endowments' of his nature.

They also reintroduced the role of fickle Fortune, which gradually changes from an idea of Providence to that of pure chance. Machiavelli cites the two ways of obtaining glory – or a principality – as *virtù* or good fortune, but goes on to stress that the prince who has *virtus* has the best chance of the help of the goddess of fortune. *Fortes fortuna adiuvat*– 'Fortune favours the brave.' In the Augustian view, success is due to 'Divine Providence' and 'Fortuna, the goddess of luck', plays no role whatsoever. Success is not achieved a brave battle against fortune.

Certainly throughout the period, there is a gradual shift from the Christian idea of one's lot being the result of the grace of God and a greater insistence on the role of man. Indeed, the stress on Greek myths and heroes gradually transformed people's values. *Virtù* gradually ceased to be a moral quality and became Machiavelli's 'prowess', something more akin to the Greek *arete* – ability or excellence in one's field – than Christian virtue.

Another factor was the effect of the Biblical studies under taken by scholars, particularly the Northern Humanists. One could even say that Biblical humanism was, as Quentin Skinner says, a Trojan Horse, undermining traditional authority by putting the Bible into the vernacular and making it accessible to everyone which clearly showed the claims of Pope and Emperor to be at variance with the original text. This undermined the claims od the Church to exercise temporal power.

As the Renaissance progressed, things had come back to

the point where a strong ruler was accepted as the best form of governance for the sake of security and peace as evidenced in Machiavelli[20] although he still hankered for the liberty of a Republic. Pier Paolo Vergerio's *On Monarchy* clearly states that 'monarchy is to be preferred to the rule of the people' although he had earlier stated that the best form was a combination of the three forms, as in the case of Venice (*Fragment on the Republic of Venice*).

It seems that the whole project of the Renaissance had been to remove God from the framework of temporal power and to lay the groundwork for secularisation. Indeed, Machiavelli attacks Christianity for subverting civic life in elevating the wrong values, e.g. 'humility, abnegation and contempt for mundane things' rather than 'magnanimity, physical strength' and things that make men bold.

NOTES

1. 'Law is the primal and ultimate mind of God' and 'the true and primal law, applied to command and prohibition, is the right reason of supreme Jupiter.' (*Laws*, I, vi. 18) The early Romans also made a distinction between *fax*, which was due to a divine command (but remained abstract and not personified as *themis*), and *jus* which God established by men. *Jus* was used comprehensively for law by the Romans.

2. 'Be the *polis* in which thy have their abode great, or be it small, men's lives are all controlled by nature (*physis*) and by *nomos*. Nature is something unordered, something uneven, something peculiar to each man; *nomoi* are something common, something ordered, something identical for all men. Nature, if it be evil, often wishes for evil things ... *nomoi* wish for the just, the good, and the beneficial.' Demonsthenes.

3. 'No single thing is so like another ... as all of us are to one another ... And so, however, we may define man, a single definition will apply to all.

4. Although the use of 'state' is an anachronism as it was not used in the modern sense until about the sixteenth century.

5. Others also assisted the Romanisation process. Tertullian, a jurist, laid out Christian doctrine in the form of legal principles. The fifth century provided Denys the Areopagite (a Syrian who tried to pass himself off as Paul's disciple) who presented a semi-philosophic

explanation for power structures in the world and invented and coined the term hierarchy (*hierarchia*).

6. This system of governance is called Caesaropapism.

7. 'There is no power but of God,' and hence only delegated power, and, in the case of the Pope, the Petrine power of loosing and binding was passed straight to him from St. Peter.

8. Both of which are Roman constitutional term. This was in fact originally a *de facto* recognition of the two powers of the Christian Church and the pagan Roman Empire.

9. Hence the later *Rex Dei Gratia* (King by the Grace of God) which started with the Lombards in Northern Italy in the late 6th century and by the 8th century was standard usage in the West.

10. Named for Gelasius, a fifth century pope. The spread of this concept in the West, a process which was set in motion by Pope Gregory (509-603) in an attempt to provide an alternative base of power against the imperial claims of Constantinople, set in motion a process by which royal law gradually usurped common law. In Walter Ullman's terms, the traditional German ascending idea of power was replaced by the democratic descending idea of power.

11. Not being as clever or pragmatic as Clovis, who adopted the Roman structure for his own ends.

12. On the other hand, the King, particularly in the English tradition, was also a feudal overlord, which involved the feudal contract – a legal bond between lord and vassal – Ullman's ascending model. Whereas the continental theocratic form later dissolved in a wave of revolution, the English variety gave rise to a theory of contractual government.

13. As did Accursius (c. 1220-60) and Alexander of Hales. Justifications like 'payment for the failure to pay' developed.

14. That this could take place is indicative of the dissolution of a 'total' unified Christian view and what Walter Ullman calls 'the atomization of man.'

15. What we are discussing here refers mainly to the Italian phenomenon. The pre-imperial Germanic peoples – and hence the English – were heirs to another constitutional tradition. Although each people was ruled by a king, the king was not absolute but owed certain things to his nobles who in turn owed him certain duties. He could not *make* law, but was bound by customary law – he could formulate, implement and enforce this custom – although a king, if powerful enough, could exceed this. The debate between the two forms was never entirely exhausted. As Bracton, an English jurist of the thirteenth century, said, 'The king himself ought to be under no man, but under God and under the law, because law makes the king. Let the king, therefore, give authority and rule to the law, seeing that these are conferred upon

the king himself by the law. For there is no king where will rules and not law.' The king ultimately came from the people, as eleventh century Manegold of Lautenbach says, 'No man can make himself emperor or king. It is the people which raises an individual above itself, that he may rule and direct it according to the principles of just government.'

16. A hot-bed of Aristotelianism at the time. He wrote his work in Paris where scholastic debates were hot and fierce, not infrequently leading to the losers having to flee elsewhere before the Church Inquisitor caught up with them.

17. It is worth taking note of the commercial banking development in this period. In the twelfth century, there were standard coinages in Italy, Norman England. Sicily and Flanders, thus enabling a credit system as accounts could be kept and letters of credit used. Christian usurers, charging 10-17%, were replacing the Jewish usurers who charged 40-50%.

As mentioned before, various lawyers and thinkers came up with legal devices to get around the laws against usury. Banks were formed by a union of merchants in a family or even a town, and then were used to control the markets. Their influence was so great that no important business transaction could take place without them (e.g. Edward III could not have begun the Hundred Years War without a loan from the Florentine bankers in London, and Emperor Charles V once borrowed 2 million in a single year). Italian bankers also made loans to Popes and prelates to consolidate their position. Florence had eighty banking houses in 1252; they used the gold florins of twenty-four carats which was the standard of value throughout Europe. The equivalent would be the modern adoption of the ecu, except that it is intrinsically worthless.

18. In fact, the only places which avoided despots were those places like Venice where a merchant oligarchy continued to dominate the scene using a republican form, which resulted in a kind of adulation of Venice.

19. In *The Crisis of the Early Italian Renaissance* (1966) and elsewhere. He stresses the role of Aristotelian ideas in the formation of humanism.

20. it is to Machiavelli that we owe the word 'state'. He wrote of '*lo stato del principe*', the state of the prince.

The Reformist Revision

The definitive separation of 'religion' from the secular comes about in the Reformation, thereby paradoxically achieving the opposite of its purported goal. Rather than elevating man's spirituality, it gave free rein to developments in the secular field, unhampered by any mediation on the part of the Church, for religion was now a matter of individual salvation, a matter of faith, conscience, and 'inner light'. Thus, as E. Troeltsch says, the Reformation:

> ...shatters the whole fabric of Catholic reconciliation in the realm of metaphysics and of ethics, as well as its doctrine of society. Out of the ruins there arises a very hard and artificial conception of life.' (*The Social Teachings of the Christian Churches*)

Latin Catholicism allots part of the Supreme authority to the Church on the earth, thus having an effect on the social realm. Protestantism makes actions external and not spiritual, and thus subject to secular power whereas belief, conviction, etc. are 'inward' and not to be encroached on by the secular authority.[1] Religion no longer intervened in social life. That was to become ultimately the prerogative of the reason or individual conscience, which was given free rein.[2]

There had always been radical ideas about sovereignty, power and its source, authority, the division between the secular and the spiritual, etc., throughout the Middle Ages -- we have already mentioned Bartolus and Marsiglio. There was also William of Ockham in England (1280?-

1349?) who limited papal power and said, 'Law is a command of will' and since it involves the consent of the people, even the Pope can be deposed. Why did this not gain popular acceptance until the Reformation? A change in *zeitgeist* must take place to make an idea catch on – this, I would suggest, is usually due to some economic impetus which is accompanied by a major social upheaval.[3] Political ideas do not exist in isolation from the society from which they spring.

But with the Reformation the idea finally took hold that all believers had authority (by Inner light), i.e. authority is **NOT** divinely conferred. Everyone has authority. But then the question had to be asked, if the idea of authority as a divinely entrusted commission goes out the window, what will take its place unless men are free to live in total lawlessness, each one subject only to his own whims and free to do entirely as he wishes, or resort to ochlocracy, mob-rule? The question must arise – why any authority at all? What is the justification?

This was the question posed by the Anabaptists once the gates of anarchy were opened by Luther. The origins of this sect go back to a split in Zürich where Conrad Grebel and George Blaurock and their followers said that infant baptism was no baptism and had themselves rebaptised. They were fiercely persecuted because they refused to conform to political authorities – and, particularly when they were allied with social causes, they aroused great hostility.[4]

The challenge to Papal, and therefore Church authority, was mirrored by a challenge to the classical authorities. This attack on the Ancients is indicative of the rising spirit of modernity. Modernity is characterised by subjectivity, i.e., by the fact that man himself serves as the measure and ground of all truth. Truth ceases to depend upon the authority of revelation and finds its ground in man's own perception and reflection. From this point man measures his being only insofar as he perceives and thinks, and the world is only insofar as it can be thought or perceived. The human being now thinks of himself as an independent being who can measure, conquer, and transform nature as he likes.

Ironically, once Luther had unwittingly opened the flood-gates of change, he himself backed down because he recognised the danger inherent in what he had so righteously, as he thought at the time, done. He said on 5 September, 1524:

> I have already said that Christians are rare in the world; therefore the world needs a strict, hard temporal government that will compel and restrain the wicked not to steal and rob and to return what they borrow, even though a Christian ought not to demand it (the principal) or even hope to get it back. This is necessary in order that the world may not become a desert, peace may not perish, and trade and society may not be utterly destroyed; all which would happen if we were to rule the world by the Gospel and not drive and compel the wicked, by laws and the use of force, to do and suffer what is right. We must, therefore, keep the roads open, preserve peace in the towns, and enforce law in the land, and let the sword hew briskly and boldly against the transgressors, as Paul teaches in Romans xii. For it is God's will that those who are not Christians shall be held in check and kept from doing usury, at least with impunity. Let none think that the world can be ruled without blood; the sword of the ruler must be red and bloody, for the world will and must be evil, and the sword is God's rod and vengeance upon it.[5]

Thus the purely secular state has become a necessity. Once the door to secularism (with its potential for acting as a tool for economic exploitation) was opened, the change in *zeitgeist* gained force from the sixteenth century. There were the extreme groups like the sixteenth century monarchomachs like the French Huguenot, François Hotman who said in *Franco-Gallia* that the king derives his power from the people, not from God and that the people are sovereign and have a right to remove a tyrant. The king is subject to the control of the people. His thesis[6] was that kings were originally elected and were not hereditary and the magistrates were elected by the people to keep an eye on the king, not to enforce his decrees. For them, ultimately even tyrannicide was acceptable.

Even monarchists like Jean Bodin[3] in 1576 in his *République* were drawn into positing the state as a non-religious association, charged with the maintenance of order. Being in the midst of a civil war, it was easy to draw such a conclusion. The state **must** have a supreme authority and which possesses power over the law – this is the beginning of the modern idea of political authority. This is a repudiation of the mixed or shared authority of the medieval ruler. It was an almost Justinian view of authority and led ultimately to the 'divine right of kings'. A ruler of this sort becomes law maker, judge and magistrate.[7] Such a view of governance could not come about until man perceived himself in a new way, in a non-religious secular context.

One cannot underestimate the impact that Calvin's legalising of usury had. His attack on the Aristotelian concept of the sterility of money has been deemed 'a turning point in the history of European thought' by some. The economic and social implications of this had far-reaching political consequences.[8] Tawney notes in *Religion and the Rise of Capitalism* that the loosening of the economic bonds of the Medieval world order was dependent on the abolition of the Canon law strictures about the prohibition of usury and other limitations on business practice. Westfall expresses it succinctly when he says, 'Economic activity shook off the guiding hand of Christian ethics and declared itself to be an independent aspect of life, governed by its own impersonal laws.'[9] Thus there is a correlation between the break-up of the traditional church order and the emergence of a new mode of being. Henry VIII of England was the first legally to permit usury.

NOTES

1. This can have a flip side in totalitarianism which the secular authority extends its power over the 'inward' (thoughts, convictions) and thus becomes a 'religious' state.

2. Interestingly enough, it was Calvinism and the theocratic state in Geneva which was the forerunner of modern democracy. Calvin said that he preferred government by the many rather than the one, thus laying the foundation for modern democracy, and in the person of Rousseau, nationalism.

3. Economically at this time, the Germans (represented fiscally by the Fuggers) had a free hand in the money market. The Medici had been expelled. The Habsburg Emperor Maximilian was completely dependent on them to solve his 'cash flow' problems. The Fuggers' main profits were based on arbitrage–transmission fees, augmented by 11% interest on loans and dealing in metals and commodities.

Their 1488 loan of 150,000 florins to the Tyrolean Archduke Sigismund netted them a profit of 40% net. Some of their loans were repaid through indulgences throughout Germany. From 1509, the representative of the house of Fugger had a key to each indulgence box – half the proceeds went to the Pope (via the Fuggers with commission) and the other half directly to the Fuggers. Indeed, the Fuggers were the bank of deposit for the Pope,

4. Paradoxically, it was popular outrage at the actions of usurers and extortioners, and the Church's tacit acceptance of the practice, that provided the fuel for the popular upheaval. At this time, there was a popular cry for the repression of usurers. (c.f. C. H. Tawney) Luther took up the cry and said, 'The greatest misfortune of the German nation is easily the traffic of interest … The devil invented it, and the Pope, by giving his sanction to it, has done untold evil throughout the world.' Luther also said that it was time 'to put a bit in the mouth of

the holy company of the Fuggers.' When Eck travelled to Italy to seek confirmation for the lawfulness of interest in merchant transactions, the Fuggers willingly financed his journey.

5. His gloomy view of human nature certainly presages that of Hobbes.

6. And that of other French Calvinists: Simon Goulert, Theodore de Bèze in *Rights of Magistrates*, G. Buchanan. There was the very famous *Vindiciae Contra Tyrannos* which posits two contracts: one people the king and the people and God, and the other between the people and the king. This removed any personal, inherited charisma from the king. This was the reasoning behind John Knox's attack on Queen Mary in Scotland.

7. Who also had a go at monopolists in 1569, explaining inflation – *La Reponse de Jean Bodin aux Paradoxes de Malestroit touchant l'enchérissement de toutes choses.*

8. When the position of the ruler was denigrated, these functions derived their authority from the secular state, rather than ultimately from God.

By the mid-century, Emperor Charles V was in trouble. Earlier (1541) he had taken loans at a maximum interest of 12% for commercial purposes. He himself borrowed heavily and surrounded himself with speculators and usurers who were reaping a nice profit from his standing debts of millions. Inflation and taxes increased and business went to the wall, yet the crown's debt continued to rise. In 1557 Spain (under Philip II) and France declared themselves bankrupt as did Portugal in 1560. Debts were converted into five per cent annuities. Various people in the Netherlands then went bankrupt. The usurers made a healthy 54% interest for sixteen years.

Debts mounted to the point where the creditors were: Nicolo di Grimaldi of Genoa, 5,000,000 ducats; Lomellino and Agostino Spinola, 1,500,000 ducats each; the Fuggers, between 3,000,000 and 4,000,000; Espinosa, 2,000,000; and Juan de Curiel de la Torre, 1,500,000.

The only real survivors of the whole nasty business were the Genoese fairs which carried on until they were replaced by Antwerp. As Davanzati, a citizen of Florence, describes them in 1581:

> The Genoese have invented a new kind of paper business which they call 'Besançon fairs' because that was their place of origin. But today they are held in Savoy, in Piedmont, in Lombardy, and in the province of Trento, outside the gates of Genoa, or indeed in any other place, so that a better name would be 'Utopia', that is to say, fairs without locality. In contrast to the Lyons fair, no merchandise is bought or sold: all that happens is that 50 or 60 bankers meet together, each with a little paper book, in order to regulate the banking business of nearly the whole of Europe and to renew it by

re-exchange at a rate of interest agreed among them, their main purpose apparently being to protract this game indefinitely. In this way they gain 250,000 scudi a year in commission alone.

9. Westfall, *Science and Religion*, p.5.

English Freedom?

The Reformation ushered in a period of embittered controversy and outright war. A large portion of subsequent political theory that was developed in England was a reaction to the chaotic conditions which existed on the continent, due to the various wars over religion, and later in England as a result of the English Civil War. This was a time of strongly held conflicting dogmatic positions. On 21 July 1542, Pope Paul III published the bull, *Licet ab initio*, which reconstituted the Holy Office of the Inquisition in Rome as the central authority for all Christendom and stated that the dogma of the Church was uniquely true and that deviance from it was dangerous and had to be extirpated (by executing the deviants and heretics with great relish).

This dogmatic feeling was not confined to Rome: in Geneva Calvin executed Michael Servetus for his unorthodox views on the Trinity. Servetus was not a revolutionary who made his views a public issue, but had written in Latin for scholars. There was, in turn, a reaction to his execution. Sebastian Castellion, writing under the name Martin Bellius, wrote *De Haereticis an sint persequendi* in 1554 against Calvin, insisting that what was important was right conduct rather than right opinions. Others, like Socinus in *De fide et operibus* and Acconcio in *Strategematum* went on to attack dogmatic systems. Their logical conclusion was that all Christian beliefs should be tolerated.[2]

In view of the conflicting positions of Catholicism and Protestantism in its various modes, the idea that the ruler must defend a particular dogma could only have one result: incessant war. On the eve of the outbreak of the Dutch

Revolt[3] and the French Wars of Religion,[4] the then French Chancellor, Michel de l'Hôpital, made a speech in 1566 in which he stated that the business of the statesman was to maintain peace and order and he is the only competent judge of that. The anarchy and bloodshed of the fighting between the Catholics and the Huguenots drove the French to resolve this, through the Edict of Nantes in 1598 which gave religious toleration to the Huguenots.[5]

The logic of this position leads to the conclusion that the state exists in its own right to guarantee peace and security and so it determines its own actions without reference to a prior spiritual authority. Having removed God from the picture of direct governance, who then would determine what was right and wrong? Man. In *The Laws of Ecclesiastical Polity*, Richard Hooker (1554-1600) stated that men have a sure guide in their rational faculty[6] and men naturally seek what is good. The universe has a perceived rational order which only needs to be discovered. Since this is the case, collective agreement is the test of the truth and so forms of law and government are determined by consent and God-given wisdom and do not have a divine origin.

The Scottish Calvinist, George Buchanan, anticipated the doctrine of natural rights in *De jure regni apud Scotos*. He held that men are by nature sociable[7] and that the highest form of association is the state when it is founded on justice. A society must have a government and it must have a popular origin. He stated that all men are by nature equal and people submit to a ruler and laws in order to obtain the advantages of reciprocal benefits:

> By the laws of nature, an equal had neither the power nor the right of assuming authority over his equals, for I think it but justice that among persons in other respects equal, the returns of command and obedience should also be equal.

The source of sovereignty was hotly debated during the Commonwealth between the Puritans and the Levellers, the Levellers claiming that the Parliament was as bad as the King. Finally on 4 January 1649, the Rump resolved:

> ...that the People are, under God, the Original of all just Power...that the Commons of England in Parliament assembled being chosen by, and representing, the People have the supreme power in this Nation.

Thomas Hobbes (1588-1679) is perhaps the real instigator of the power of the modern state. Man is *not* a sociable creature, not naturally disposed to good, but rather to seek power and gain. Men are all equal and their natural rights only limited by their individual strengths.[8] In such a state, a man could get and keep anything he had the power to keep, thus obliging constant warfare. He states: 'the Value, or Worth of a man, is as of all things, his Price; that is to say, so much as would be given for the use of his Power,' (Lev. p. 151) or 'The manifestation of the Value we set on one another is that which is commonly called Honouring.' (p. 152) It is at this point, at the very beginning of the modern concept of human relations which are couched in economic terms, that the market economy we see today became inevitable. Indeed, the doctrine of market forces is already laid out, as Hobbes says, 'The value of all things contracted for is measured by the Appetite of the Contractors; and therefore the just value, is that which they are contented to give.' (p. 208)

Men come together in a social contract for self preservation from a state of constant anxiety and strife. The state now becomes a negative concept, a principle of control – for the defence and protection of the individuals, their persons and their property, not for wisdom, truth, virtue or happiness.

This is more than Consent, or Concord; it is a reall

Unitie of them all, in one and the same Person, made by Covenant of every man with every man, in such manner, as if every man should say to every man, I *Authorise and give up my Right of Governing my selfe, to this Man, or to this Assembly of men, on this condition, that thou give up thy Right to him, and Authorise all his Actions in like manner.* This done, the Multitude so united in one Person, is called a COMMON-WEALTH, in latine CIVITIS. This is the Generation of that great LEVIATHAN... For by this Authoritie, given him by every particular man in the Common-Wealth, he hath the use of so much Power and Strength conferred on him, that by terror thereof inabled to forme the wills of them all, to Peace at home, and mutuall ayd against their enemies abroad...

And he that carryeth this Person, is called SOVERAIGNE, and said to have *Soveraigne Power;* and every one besides, his SUBJECT.

The function of the state becomes the maintenance of the freedoms of the contract, labour, exchange, and capital accumulation. Its job is to preserve the market from anarchy. Political stability means optimum conditions for stable capital growth and debt collection. The desire for gain and increase underlies all. Greed is a powerful stimulant and is itself stimulated by the system. Indeed, the system runs on greed. Greed is the lubricant. That which was previously a sin becomes an asset.

This state has total power, complete and absolute, to make and enforce laws in all areas.[9] Once established, a sovereign could not be resisted or opposed. The law was nothing more than the sovereign's will, so nothing should limit or restrain it.

There was now a language and doctrine of the state. Other thinkers followed a similar line, like Samuel von Pufendorf (1632-1694) who agreed with the Hobbesian doctrine of empirical state government by rule of law, but not with his conclusions about human nature.[10]

Another defender of absolutism was Sir Robert Filmer in *Patriarcha* who went so far as to say that it was against nature for subjects to challenge the authority of their kings.[11] He asserted that kings had paternal power which had been granted them by God. This is really an attempt to resuscitate the theocratic vision of the state.

Spinoza, after seeing the absolutist Louis IX inflict defeat on the republic of the Netherlands, concluded in his unfinished *Tractatus politicus*, 'the function of the State is purely and simply to guarantee peace and security; it follows that the best State is that in which men live their lives in concord and in which their rights are inviolate.' Thus the individual is granted his freedom of thought, that freedom and the security of the individual being **guaranteed** by the State.

Rationalism and a trust in science were beginning to dominate the scene, although the thinkers were all Christian and believed in God as the Creator of the universe. Things were approached 'scientifically' in the naive belief that this would make the human race better. Leibniz was representative of this trend, while being perhaps unique at the time in recognising the potential dangers in the presumptions behind rationalism, telling the rationalists that they 'were preparing everything for the general revolution with which Europe is threatened.' These words were directed against John Locke.

All these writers were justifying a strong and powerful state, largely as a response to actual events, and stressed the existence of a social contract as involved in its establishment.

This development centred on England and Holland, and gave rise to liberalism, espoused by the middle classes who felt that extremism was bad for business. Being middle-class and entrepreneurial, the theocratic view was unpopular, as it threatened proprietary rights. Economic interest was dominant.[12]

John Locke became the guiding light of political thought

in the eighteenth century, and he and his *Treatises of Civil Government* are associated with the victory of William of Orange. He wanted to refute the absolutist position of Filmer's *Patriarcha*. He said that Adam was **not** a divinely appointed monarch. Adam had no absolute rights over Eve or his descendants. When a child reaches maturity, then parental authority ends. His contention is that if Filmer is right, every man is born a slave. For Locke, every man is born free, as he states in the second treatise, that all men are originally in 'a state of perfect freedom to order their actions and dispose of their <u>possessions</u>.' (II.ii.4) Furthermore, man, by his rational faculty, can know the fundamental principles of morality, but men are partial.

The remedy for this is a civil government in which men (of property) consent to form a social contract and create a polity. The contract is **not** between ruler and ruled, but between all men.

Men being, as has been said, by nature all free, equal, and independent, no one can be put out of this estate, and subjected to the political power of another, without his own consent. The only way by which any one divests himself of his natural liberty and puts on the bonds of civil society is by agreeing with other men to join and unite into a community for their comfortable, safe, and peaceable living one amongst another, in a secure enjoyment of their properties, and a greater security against any that are not of it...

For when any number of men have, by the consent of every individual, made a community, they have thereby made that community one body, with a power to act as one body, which is only by the will and determination of the majority...

And thus every man, by consenting with others to make one body politic under one government, puts himself under an obligation to every one of that society, to submit to the determination of the majority, and to be concluded by it... (II.viii.95- 97)

Thus government, as he said, 'has no other end but the preservation of property,'[13] (II.vii.90) and sovereignty rests with the people and actions must be taken according to the will of the majority and then everyone is bound by that. As a balance, he also advanced the separation of powers. Also, as the spokesman for Whig constitutionalism, he stated that rebellion against a ruler who broke the law was legitimate and necessary.[14]

His ideas were influential and prepared the way for modern popular governments and the spread of the penchant for majority rule and the division of executive, legislative and judicial powers. Perhaps even more influential were his liberal ideas.[15] Voltaire was very enthusiastic about Locke and took his ideas to France where their impact was devastating. Although Locke regards the existence of God in his picture as necessary and implicit, he does consider what man is like without God: 'If man were independent he could have no law but his own will, no end but himself. He would be a god to himself and the satisfaction of his own will the sole measure and end of all his actions.'

NOTES

1. Calvin said, 'Usury is not now unlawful, except in so far as it contravenes equity and brotherly union.'
2. Bodin included all people with belief – Jews, Muslims, philosophers and sceptics (because of their grasp of natural law) in the *Heptaplomeres* which is unique in its time. However, Bodin did not dare publish it and it only existed in manuscripts.
3. 1568-1648 in which the Dutch Protestants tried to break free from the imposed Catholicism of Philip II.
4. 1562-1598 between the rival Catholic faction, led by the Guise family and supported by the regent, Catherine de Medici, and the Calvinist faction, led by the Coligny brothers and Bourbon King of

Navarre. France later also entered the Thirty Years War.

5. The Huguenot Henry IV of Navarre had resolved the situation by becoming Catholic to obtain the crown.

6. This was contrary to the Calvinist position that man's reason and will were both corrupted by the Fall of Man. He said that only the will was corrupted. Hooker was much quoted by John Locke.

7. Like Aristotle.

8. This is the beginning of the insistence on the individual and his freedoms.

9. It should be noted that Hobbes was also a mathematician who thought that human relationships could be accurately described in empirical terms.

10. In the *Discourses Concerning Government*, Algernon Sidney said that no one ever alienated all his natural rights to a sovereign. Subjects could rebel, but it was better to set up a limited government.

11. French writers were giving the sovereign a divine origin, like Bossuet in *Politics drawn from the very words of Holy Scripture*. The Edict of Nantes was also revoked in 1685.

12. Of course, the lower classes were simply 'morally depraved' and were incapable of exercising political rights since they lacked rationality (and property!).

13. The economic interest of property was a dominant theme in Locke.

14. War at this time consumed vast sums of money. The War of the Spanish Succession (1701-1713) involved ALL the major European powers. (There were also the War of the League of Augsburg (1688-1697), Louis XIV's expansionist wars, Irish resistance to William, the Great Northern War). The lenders made vast sums of money. Isaac Suasso advanced William of Orange 2,000,000 florins, and during the war, we have Marlborough's troops supported by Sir Solomon Medina and Joseph Cortisos, while Louis XIV was supported by Jacob Worms. By the time of Louis' death, France's finances were in a parlous state which opened the way to the introduction of paper money by John Law with his modern ideas of credit, saying that, for a merchant, hard cash or credit were the same.

In England, financial straits impelled the government to grant the right of setting up the Bank of England in return for the capital of £1,200,000 being lent to the government. The Bank had the right to deal in precious metals and foreign bills of exchange and to issue paper money.

Back in France, Law's ideas extended further and gained acceptance. Initially, the notes were issued against secure assets, but success led to a Banque Royale which granted credits to the State without collateral. When the first payment of interest fell due, the currency collapsed. It was the first step in a long drama of collapse which put the French off banks for some time. It also led to the South Sea Bubble in England.

15. *Letter on Toleration.*

'Enlightened' Ideas

A mention of the 'Enlightenment' would not be complete without Descartes (d. 1650). By 1700, Cartesianism had become generally accepted. It posited a mechanistic, ordered universe and man as a mechanical body with an immortal soul. 'The Enlightenment attempts to replace what we may call the metaphysical absolute by the absolute certainty of effective solutions to practical problems,'[1] or an attempt to capture the absolute in a methodological net. The backbone of Descartes' approach was analytic reasoning based on empirical evidence. Descartes' revolutionary re-interpretation of man and of the world is represented in the formula *Ego cogito ergo sum* ('I think therefore I am') as self-consciousness. Man thinks of himself as an independent being who can measure, conquer, and transform nature, thus becoming something in and for himself, capable of establishing laws and judging both man and nature as the basis of himself alone. 'Modern' man consequently becomes free in a hitherto unknown way and sets out to liberate the world from superstition and error and to re-found social and political institutions upon man himself.

Such analysis led Spinoza to subject the Old Testament to reasoning and conclude that the prophecy and miracles in it were nothing more than human superstition and credulity.[2] Eventually it led many to completely jettison religion as irrational superstition.[3] Following Descartes, no received knowledge was acceptable unless it conformed to reason. Furthermore, to be modern was to write in modern European languages, not Latin; to follow Descartes, not Aristotle; to accept Copernicus, not Ptolemy.[4]

The first of the new breed, the *philosophes*, Bernard de

Fontenelle (1657-1757), was instrumental in popularizing the new view. Newton succeeded Descartes in popularity and his view was equally uniform and law-abiding, but he introduced an *invisible* force, gravity, which Cartesians found hard to grasp. Locke had added to this with his *Essay Concerning Human Understanding,* which said that the human mind was a blank slate which had ideas imprinted on it by sensation.[5] This replaced reason with experience. Nothing is clearly perceived as it is, but only in the form of an idea.[6] There was also a move from general reason to particular facts and a dislike of all dogma. Locke and Pierre Bayle condemned all metaphysics because such knowledge was beyond human capacity.[7]

Montesquieu, in the *Spirit of the Laws*, went on to describe how various societies order their politics. Basing himself on Lockean psychology, he shows how the laws of a society are moulded by circumstances. Thus laws are not abstract rules, but rather relationships – and hence relative, not absolute. When looking at classical civilization, the point was that they saw that a peaceful society full of virtue could exist without Christianity. Diderot, an atheist, also pointed out that morality was relative. Hence no one had a monopoly of truth and hence **all** must be tolerated. Toleration became the supreme political virtue[8] – as long as it did not conflict with 'enlightened' principles.

Montesquieu divided government into republics, monarchies and despotisms.[9] He thought republics the most admirable, but least workable, effective only when they were small and then they were too small to resist larger powers (with the exception of the Dutch Republic).[10] Their guiding spirit was virtue. Monarchy, for him, was the government of one man according to law, tempered by intermediary bodies (like the nobility or magistrates or parliaments). Its guiding spirit was honour. A despotism, whose guiding spirit was fear, was ruled by will, not by law.[11] Mind you, it was noted that despots got things done, so an 'enlightened' one would, in theory, be an excellent idea – rulers like Joseph II of Austria, Catherine of Russia, Frederick of Prussia, etc. The *philosophes* were very committed to getting things done.

This was very seductive when people had social programmes they felt had to be undertaken, and no government was so bold as to undertake them. Le Mercier de la Rivière in 1767 (*The Natural and Essential Order of Political Societies*) suggested that what was needed was *legal* despotism, the rule of one man who ruled according to the law of nature.[12]

There was a change from flexible reasonableness to an intransigent, dogmatic rationalism. The central figure in this shift was Baron Henri d'Holbach (1723-1789). His position was taken up by people like Diderot and Priestley. They all wrote on moral or political liberty and natural necessity, stressing the latter. Constitutional freedom gave way to the infallible will or the law of nature. That which did not conform was condemned. Codification was the rage.

Given a mechanistic view of the world, they thought it was simply necessary to enact the proper rules and to teach people, even against their will, how to behave in order to make them 'happy' and 'prosperous',[13] how to *impose* freedom and happiness on them – such a line of thought would also lead eventually to totalitarian democracy and bloodshed. For to follow this line of thought, if you were not enlightened then you were in ignorance. Once you had become enlightened, you became reified – you became a rational object. Thus the freedom of modern science is mere rhetoric, for once you are an object, freedom has no meaning.

The end of the experiment of 'enlightened despots' supposedly acting out the principles of the *philosophes* – or rather playing at being *philosophes* – was not a pleasant sight:

Now reality takes over. The armies that march are real armies; cities are put to the torch; the Irish cotters starve to death by the thousand, and in Russia Empress Catherine and Emperor Paul add millions to the number of serfs and state peasants. Negroes are kidnapped on the coasts of Africa and transported to the New World, rotting in the noisome holds of slave ships; the Church hunts down heretics and destroys them…That is the real world, long after Frederick and Catherine and Joseph and Gustavus have had their day.

The comedy is over, and reality take charges. …In the end it is 'infuriated man seeking through blood and slaughter his long-lost liberty,'[14] seeking and not finding. For in the end the philosophers were not kings at all: Turgot dismissed, Necker dismissed, Tanucci dismissed, Count Rumford expelled by the dissolute Karl Theodore, the mighty Pombal disgraced, Struense beheaded, Gustavus himself murdered, Lord Edward Fitzgerald betrayed and killed, Priestley mobbed and driven into exile, Brissot guillotined, Condorcet dead in that jail in Bourge l'Égalité, a copy of Horace in his pocket. The few who survived in power – Sonnenfels in Vienna, Pitt in London, for example, conveniently forgot most of their liberal opinions for, like their masters, they were frightened out of their wits by the spectacle of reforms translated from philosophy to politics.[15]

The political results of the Enlightenment are inevitable, as Rosen says:

'In sum, the historical individual is torn apart by the process of Enlightenment. Universal form contains an infinitely self-contradictory content, which in turn negates, instead of being synthesized by, that form. The direct political result is the French Revolution: the universal principle of freedom with the content of the Terror. Negativity is also the force of work or production however: out of Robespierre, it generates Napoleon.'[16]

The legacy of the Enlightenment was the rhetorical focus on individual freedom and the effort to construct a system of values based entirely on it. Rationalists had reduced liberty and particularly to logical functions of rational systems. There was a huge emphasis on science – most of the major figures at least dabbled in something scientific – and the rational systemization of knowledge. The three key themes of the Enlightenment were: Reason, Nature and Progress. Progress was a new idea – the idea that man can develop in such a way as to make himself and society better.[17]

What has actually happened is that the intellect has resolved that the will shall be god and hence man will not only master and control nature, he will reconstitute it according to his will. In fact, the 'liberal' ideas of the Enlightenment lead to tyranny – in form, structure, rules, universality which entails suppression of disagreement – which is called 'ignorance' and 'superstition'. Taken to its logical conclusion, opposition to 'the rational Truth' must be suppressed and all must become homogenised in the universal.[18]

Initially, the Enlightenment spawned four children – Rousseau and his naturalism, Bentham and utilitarianism, Kant and idealism, and Lamarck and evolutionism.[2] And we are still experiencing the effects of it today. Most of what passes today as post-Enlightenment is, in fact, the Enlightenment in yet another guise. The demotion of the intellect in favour of the will continues to reverberate. As Rosen observes:

> Despite the the exaltation of mathematical and experimental science as the mediate source of power, modern philosophy *demotes* the intellect by making it instrumental to the will. In so doing, it necessarily *promotes* what from the classical standpoint is the lower

part of the soul, Modern man wills to be free because he cannot accept restraints upon his passions or desires. In the metaphorical language of (genuine) Platonism, he rejects the Ideas as restraints upon Eros. Wonder, or awe in the presence of the divine, is replaced by curiosity...

NOTES

1. Stanley Rosen, *Hermeneutics as Politics*, p. 145.

2. His conclusion (in *Theologico-Political Treatise*) was that the point of theology was not truth, but obedience for the sake of political tranquillity. He was followed by the French Oratorian, Simon, who, after scutinising the Old Testament, turned his analysis to the New Testament with equal scorn.

3. Did not Descartes say, 'the use of our free will ... renders us in a way like God, by making us masters of ourselves'?

4. It logically led to rejection of traditional Christianity, although no one was admitting it. Those who tried to reconcile Cartesianism and Christianity, like Leibniz and Malebranche, were ridiculed. Also in positing a mathematical approach to 'truth', scientific rationality inevitably – and quite logically – leads to domination and tyranny because morality, innate or otherwise, is mathematically meaningless.

5. Meaning that souls were born without the idea of God. He also states that ideas of good and bad arose from sensations of pain or pleasure, not from an innate moral sense. He also denied original sin, the literalness of the scriptures and the trinity.

6. Berkeley went on to remove matter from the equation, saying that matter has existence only by being perceived by an observer. Others went the materialist route, eliminating mind.

7. A dogmatic statement in itself!

8. In the arena of religion, 'Natural Religion' and deism became the order of the day – religion based on the harmony of nature and sociability of men. Religion should be based on reason. Criticism accelerated, leaving Christianity with very little except good will and benevolence. Montesquieu regarded religion as an invention of the few to regulate the many. Some, like Thomas Paine, rejected Christianity. Among the more conservative, deism was popular – God the Creator who then left the universe to run itself based on rational laws.

9. *Esprit des lois* (1748), II, ch. 1.

10. Who more than made up for their lack of size with their economic clout.

11. He did get a whiff of what could result from a purely secular vision. In *Les Lettres Persanes* (84), he says, 'That makes me think that justice is

eternal and does not depend upon human conventions; if it depended on them, that would be a terrible truth which one must hide from oneself.'

12. Terms like 'absolutism' and 'enlightened despotism' were invented by the nineteenth century looking back.

13. For instance, G.G. Lamprecht of Halle set out to find a program for Prussia which would make the citizens 'more well-behaved, healthier, wiser, richer and more secure.' The measures to be employed involved things like making all towns precisely the same size, streets and roads to meet at right angles, and forbidding the colouring of Easter eggs.

14. Thomas Jefferson, First Inaugural Address.

15. Henry Steele Commager, *The Empire of Reason*, pp. 117-118 (1978).

16. Stanley Rosen, *Hermeneutics as Politics*, p. 95.

17. It was especially espoused by Turgot and Condorcet.

18. This is the New World Order par excellence, a logical development of the Enlightenment. The heavy-handed imposition of the prevailing democratic ideology, market forces, etc. is entirely 'logical' and 'rational'. As Rosen says:

'...philosophy is by nature immoderate. A rigorous and consistent defense of the Enlightenment, or the thesis that freedom is the highest good and scientific knowledge its most powerful instrument, leads in principle to what Kojève called the universal and homogeneous state. It leads to the suppression and indeed the exclusion of error and superstition. But whereas there are many forms of error and superstition, there is only one form of scientific truth – or so the Enlightenment claimed.' (p. 138)

German Idealism

If France was to become the fount of revolution[1] and England the home of economic theory, empiricism and utilitarianism, Germany came to dominate metaphysics[2] and the arts.[3]

Gotthold Lessing and Immanuel Kant were the bridges here. Lessing stayed within the bounds of the rational Enlightenment or *Aufklärung* and its *philosophes* until 1780 when, in *The Education of Humanity*, he called for the internalization of the moral unity of mankind within each individual. Kant stated in the *Critique of Judgment* that the next stage of thought beyond the Enlightenment is Metaphysics. Kant took the view that evolutionary political change was leading to perfect freedom.[4]

German 'idealism' takes its name from the position that the world we know is a product of ideas or the Mind.[5] This is the view that reality is the self-unfolding of the infinite Absolute, spontaneously and inevitably in which the finite ego disappears. It is the conceptual and systematic reconstruction and articulation of something dynamic – reliving the process through reflection. Hegel was later to hold that the Universe knows itself in and through the mind of man. Its goal was to infuse spiritual ideals into all realms of action.

One of the next stages which occurred, mainly in Germany, rejected the rationalism of the Enlightenment while taking what it could from it, is Pre-romanticism. In Britain, it is associated with Edmund Burke[6] and William Blake,[7] and in Germany with Johann Herder, Johann von Goethe and Friedrich von Schiller. They revived the emotional, pietest and mystical currents which had been stifled and were also, in part, a reaction against the very Frenchness of the Enlightenment. The German writers of *Sturm und Drang* rejected the idea that the 'enlightenment' of the human mind would ensure progress.

There was a substantial change in the idea of the individual. In the Enlightenment, individuals were considered equal to one another other and commensurate with one other, with common interests, equally necessary and valid for all in equal measure. The pre-romantics reacted to this and thought of individuals as each being unique and incommensurable with one another in any essential way. They stressed the escape from commonality into self-discovery. They reacted against the *philosophe* tendency to reduce people to interchangeable cogs who all shared in a common liberty to reason with common universal rights as being incompatible with true freedom, which was concerned with individual genius. As Schiller said, 'Every individual human soul that develops its powers is more than the greatest of human societies.' The critical, analytic and scientific is replaced by creative imagination. The artistic genius replaces the *philosophe,* the artist-warrior replaces the philosopher-soldier. What we have is the self-creating hero. The rational will becomes the non-rational will, but we are still in the Enlightenment agenda because it is the human will which is still paramount.

Johann Fichte (1762-1814),[8] Kant's disciple, stated that Absolute Being was Light which divides itself into Being and Thought. Being itself is never divided. This Being is objectified in the form of the world,[9] although the Absolute can never be grasped by the human intellect. He goes on to state[10] that 'only one Being exists purely through itself, God ...And neither within him nor outside him can a new being arise,' and the only thing external to God is the picture of Being itself, which is 'God's Being outside his Being,' the divine self-externalization in consciousness. Thus for Fichte, all the theory of science amounts to the picturing of God. No 'enlightened' Frenchman would ever have taken such a line of thought.

This line of thought, while seemingly attractive, can also lead into a dead-end. As Rosen observes about the thinking of the Idealist:

> In this case, the Absolute becomes a project or hypothesis that can never be fulfilled; we are left with finite empirical activity that motivates itself or exhibits a historical spontaneity to which a salutary but finally empty interpretation is given. The Absolute becomes the ideal completion of history, accessible only in a dream. As such, it is easily jettisoned by those hardheaded thinkers who seek to awaken the human race to the realities of scientific mastery of nature. The Absolute deteriorates first into the (Hegelian) end of history, then into the ideal of scientific progress, and finally into mere flux: mere *différance*.[11]

Fichte translated his metaphysics into political theory. When dealing with freedom, he points out that it is inseparable from law.[12] 'Rights' come into being through mutual recognition. Having the 'right' to exercise powers presupposes a community with individual wills united into a single will. Private property or individual rights have no meaning outside a social context. So the stability of rights rests on common recognition, reciprocal loyalty and trust. Given human nature, one cannot guarantee this, so there must be some power to enforce respect for rights which has been freely established – hence the contract. This is the union of all wills into one which is the General Will embodied in the State[13] (the 'union-compact'). He does not regard the State as an end in itself, but a means of fostering moral development. The State is an expression of freedom.

Fichte rejects despotism and democracy, stating 'No State may be ruled either despotically or democratically.'[14] By democracy, he means direct rule by the whole people – so there is no authority to compel people to observe its own laws. He said that there should be a tribunal (without legislative or executive powers) to ensure the authority was following the law. If it was not, it could be suspended. He also outlines a self-sufficient planned and balanced economy.[15] Fichte also stressed the cultural and linguistic unity of the German people, saying that they were the original European race, the *Urfolk*, because they had kept their original language (*Ursprache*).[16]

The intellectual leader of the *Sturm und Drang* was Johann Gottfried Herder (1744-1803). He attacked the Enlightenment and its conception of the human mind and personality, its theory of language, and its approach to poetry, the arts and history. He did not go along with splitting the mind up into compartments of will, reason, etc. He said that the human being is a total, unitary personality: 'the inner man, with all his dark forces, stimuli and impulses, is simply one.'[17] He stressed the metaphysical idea of *Kraft* which is an energy which gives man dynamic unity. It is inexplicable. In the historical area, he stressed individual cultures and the idea of the *Volk* as a genetic, developing, creative unity, even though he did not endow the *Volk* with ultimate sovereignty. Herder's concept led to ethnic-linguistic rather than territorial nationalism and had great influence in Eastern Europe.[18]

Pre-romanticism had various corollaries. First was the stress on passion and emotion not as stemming from sensations, but from the whole person. So the emotions supplied the psychic unity in a fragmented world of reason. There is, of course, a basic and obvious flaw in this. Unleashing the passions also guarantees the triumph of ignorance, since the passions cannot tolerate ANY restrictions, least of all rational ones. Thus the rationalist will to power is will on the way to becoming the unrestrained will to power. This is not Platonic divine madness. As we stated, both rationalist and reactive romanticism are spawned by the Enlightenment.

Second is the idea that the inward life of the individual and the resolution of conflict within him was then expressed in the outer world – the microcosm and the macrocosm.[19]

Thirdly it extended beyond the individual to the culture-nation (Herder) and party (Burke).[20] Thus the association becomes an extension of its individuals and an embodiment of general principle. This would eventually lead to Hegel's theory.

Hegel visualized the divine Spirit, manifested through the consciousness of man as the World-Spirit (*Weltgeist*) which is attempting to become free. In fact, all of history consists of the Idea of Freedom trying to realise itself. The unit in this development is the national spirit of a people, *Volksgeist*, which is embodied in the State. Each State is a moment in the life of the *Weltgeist* and each nation has only one epoch in which it can act at its zenith, after which it declines.

The state is like a super-organism in which the members have only the same preferences of the larger unit and this being subsumed in the state is, for Hegel, freedom: 'For Law is the objectivity of Spirit; volition in its true form. Only that will which obeys law is free; for it obeys itself – it is independent and free.'[21]

It is sort of an idealized *polis* or Roman republic, but more. According to Hegel, it is the highest form of reality, it is the Divine Idea on earth. Hegel rejected the liberal view of freedom, that man is free to do what he likes without interference as long as others can do the same, as being negative, abstract or wilful. Freedom is submitting passions to the control of reason. The existence of civil society is based on the force of the state which educated them into seeing the rationality and necessity of the state. The mystery of the state is the logic of *Aufhebung,* overcoming the individual will in favour of the universal. Pivotal to this is Hegel's idea of the completion or fulfilment of history – the culmination of the negative dialectic – 'the absolute goal of History'.[22]

NOTES

1. See next chapter.

2. Particularly flowering in the nineteenth century. We find Kant, Fichte, Schelling, Hegel, and the materialist reaction, Schopenhauer, and finally Nietzsche. Being was taken up again by Martin Heidegger in the twentieth century.

3. e.g. in music, Haydn, Mozart and later Beethoven and in theatre, *Sturm und Drang* with Goethe, Schiller, Herder (theory), et al and later Weimar Classicism.

4. Of course, in willing freedom, we are in fact imagining freedom, which means that we are empowering the imagination. In other words, to reason is to interpret, since 'logical' reason is an interpretation itself, and so reason is unreasonable.

5. It also tried to overcome the inherent subject-object separation and uneasiness which arises from perpetual and inevitable dissatisfaction in English empiricism.

6. Burke's aesthetics influenced *Sturm und Drang* via Lessing and Moses Mendolssohn.

In Germany, Mendolssohn latched on to the fact that the ideas of the Enlightenment could put Jews on an equal footing with the Christians. Moses Mendolssohn (172901786) was the organiser of the Jewish Enlightenment and his main followers were Hartwig Wessely and David Friedländer (son-in-law of the foremost Jewish banker in Berlin, David Itzig). Mendolssohn was close with Lessing, encouraging him to write *Nathan the Wise.* Count Mirabeau visited Berlin and met Mendolssohn, who explained the Jewish question to him, and he returned to France to encourage recognition of the Jews there, which finally took place in 1791. It is ironic that Mendolssohn's two daughters and his son all became Christians.

7. Coleridge was strongly influenced by it and it led him to a position which has been described as a precursor to Heidegger. As he writes, 'I would make a pilgrimage to the Deserts of Arabia...to find the man who could make [men] understand how the *one can be many*! Eternal universal mystery! It seems as if it were impossible; yet it is – & it is everywhere! – It is indeed a contradiction in Terms; and only in Terms! – It is the co-presence of Feeling & Life, limitless by their very essence, with Form,

by its very presence limited – determinate – definite –' *Notebooks*, 1:1561.

8. Schlegel points out Fichte's *Wissenschaftslehre* as one of the three parents of Romanticism along with the French Revolution and Goethe's *Wilhelm Meister*.

9. In *The Way to the Blessed Life or the Doctrine of Religion* (1806) he says that God is absolute Being and hence infinite Life as 'Being and Life are one and the same'. This Life manifests itself externally through consciousness which is the existence (*Dasein*) of God. Consciousness, the divine *Dasein*, is consciousness of Being and Being itself is beyond human comprehension.

10. *The Theory of Science in its General Outline* (1810).

11. Stanley Rosen, *The Ancients and the Moderns*, p. 77.

12. 'When you think yourself as free, you are compelled to think your freedom as falling under a law; and when you think this law, you are compelled to think yourself as free. Freedom does not follow from the law any more than the law follows from freedom. They are not two ideas, of which the one can be thought as dependent on the other, but they are one and the same idea; it is a complete synthesis.'

13. Rousseau's influence can be seen here.

14. Fichte, *Sämmtliche Werke*, III, p. 180.

15. Some consider his view to be early national socialism.

16. The Volkstum ideology was stimulated by the depredations of Napoleon.

17. *Sämmtliche Werke*, VIII, p. 179

18. Whereas Rousseau's political nationalism was influential in the West. Thus in France we see no demand for French-speaking Swiss or Belgians to join with France, nor in Netherlands any demand for the Flemish to join with the Dutch.

19. Particularly Goethe.

20. Where freely thinking men agree on broad principles.

21. *Philosophy of History*, p. 39.

22. Of course, this begs the question of what happens when the process is perfected or finished. In the twentieth century, Kojève (followed by Foucault and many other Frenchmen) views this as the death of the Spirit and hence the death of 'man' as *homo sapiens*. Human beings are then transformed into peaceful brutes who pass their time in art, sport, and *eros*. Stanley Rosen observes:

> 'Those who insist on purifying the ambiguous erotic conversations between gods and mortals into a universal and homogeneous discourse produce neither gods nor mortals but a hermeneutic of bestiality and hence neither discourse nor silence, but inarticulate noise. This is a process that will be expedited rather than stopped

by the technological 'Westernizing' of the African and Asian continents.' *Hermeneutics as Politics*, pp. 94-95.

Rousseau and Revolution

The true springboard of modern political consciousness was the child of Geneva, Jean-Jacques Rousseau. In his view, the people worship themselves as the source of all sovereignty – it is the people themselves that are the new sovereign. It is 'the will of the people' that is paramount. Indeed, in his view, the general will is always on the right track as it is morally right.[1] This is the common end of a community, not individual projects. The subjects have become citizens, and hence we have the elevation of the nation-state, based on the identity of the people or their awareness of interests held in common which forms this bond. But how can there be a multiplicity of views without men infringing each other's freedom?

Rousseau's solution was to have a small state and a homogeneous society. His ideal will not work in a large state.[2] The people of a system should have much the same customs, manners and political ideas so that it will be a cohesive community, for, according to him, man is not intrinsically moral or rational, but becomes so as he becomes a social being. For him, man is perfectible and the government should make people virtuous – so the idea of progress arises.[3]

Rousseau brought politics into the social domain, or rather brought it to bear upon the individual in a way it had not done since the Athenians. As authority, in the modern society, is self-imposed, the focus falls on each individual to state his views. The idea of a social contract or a mixed government was not new, but what he did do was to exalt political rights to an *essential* human liberty, thus the continuous participation of all citizens in the exercise of political power becomes a fundamental right of man. The idea of consent is fundamental, but the idea of the 'homogeneous' society was to have bloody consequences with the Revolution.

For the eighteenth century thinkers, particularly the French, accustomed as they were to absolutism, diversity of views was not essential[4] – what was stressed was unity and unanimity in order to achieve the 'natural' order which would lead to virtue.[5] And, of course, THE truth was embodied in scientific progress. Rousseau reacted against this and preferred Spartan virtue.[6]

Another point lay in Rousseau's comments about private property. Rousseau said that the first man to enclose land and make his neighbours think that it was legal became the source of all wars, evil and demoralization. It was the root cause of all evil[7] and an instrument to make the poor accept exploitation.[8] This led people like Abbé Morelly to become complete communists in the search for absolute equality. In the *Code de la Nature*, published in 1755, Morelly says:

> Nothing belongs wholly to anyone. Property is detestable, and anyone who attempts to re-establish it shall be imprisoned for life, as a dangerous madman and an enemy of humanity. …All produce shall be gathered into public garners, to be distributed to citizens for their subsistence. All cities shall be built on the same plan; all private residences shall be alike. All children shall be taken from their families at five years of age, and educated on a uniform plan.

What was stressed was egalitarian social harmony expressed in the demand for restricting the size of property and condemning the rising industrial civilization. Abbé Mably who wanted large fortunes broken up and redistributed with state control of trade and maintained that mediocrity was the greatest strength and to this end the state must regulate the heart of the citizen.

A major spokesman for the Revolution was Abbé Sieyes and his political pamphlet, *Qu'est-ce que le Tiers État?*, whose effect was delayed until the Revolution itself. He postulated a rational regime in place of 'meaningless' traditions.[9] He wanted to abolish privileges and raise (logically) the homogeneous nation to the only real political entity. It is a renunciation of pragmatism and tradition in favour of a pure system based on reason, exemplifying the 'Enlightened' Revolutionary attitude. The 'veritable social order' will be realized when the will of the people becomes the sole source of law, then all established laws are null and void, since they will no longer be necessary as everyone will be the same.

When the Estates General met in 1789, he wanted the Third Estate to become Rousseau's people – to start the business of a true social contract. For Sieyès, the people without privileged position *were* the nation and the aristocrats were merely aliens. It was a vision of a monolithic nation with unlimited popular sovereignty. To maintain this monolithic quality, all nonconforming elements must be eliminated. The basis of social order is equality, which is happiness, and people must be forced to it. However, he did recognise private property, in almost Lockean terms, as a natural right and the differences in it arise from activity or passivity.[10] The single-mindedness of such a rational and logical order was to lead to Jacobean terror.

What then about the non-conformist? – for his fate one has only to see the number of heads that rolled to the cry of '*Liberté, equalité, fraternité*' or the fate of the thousands executed in the wake of the Vendée Revolt. Saint-Just's comments (based on Rousseau) about different parties is chilling:

> Every party is therefore criminal, because it makes for the isolation of the people and the popular societies, and

for the independence of the government, Any faction is therefore criminal, because it neutralizes the power of public virtue.

Robespierre could not abide parties either: 'There are no other citizens in a Republic than republicans. Royalists … conspirators are nothing but aliens, or rather enemies.' Citizens are only those who spiritually identify with the nation. Furthermore, anyone who held himself aloof from the unity was immoral.[11] This was the *volonté une* of Robespierre. Ultimately he put all power in a committee[12] – 'faithful and ruthless' – a dictatorship based on the infallibility of the enlightened few. For him, 'Terror was justice,' an 'emanation of virtue.'[13] Obedience became freedom. There was a ban on the slightest difference of opinion or feeling which might show deviation from the one will – the one truth.[14]

Robespierre's monolithic vision was embraced by François-Noel Babeuf[15] who became the apostle of egalitarian communism. The Social Contract should preserve natural equality and it was the state which must undertake this task. His comrade, Philippe-Michel Buonarroti, said that 'liberty resides in the power of the sovereign,' which means the will of the people as sovereign. It is a somewhat crude version of Marx's class struggle – history is the story of avarice founded on private property.

For the Babouvists, the Terror was a justifiable means to achieve social transformation which would lead to happiness, which really amounted to an *'honnête médiocrité'*.[16] To each according to his needs, which must be equal and modest. The state **must** organise production, distribution and consumption.[17] All are employees, pensioners and producers of the state. As there is no private property, it being owned by the State, labour is the individual's contribution.

The Babouvist definition of democracy is very revealing. Democracy is now a system where all citizens contribute to the formation of laws and does not mean universal franchise. Democracy is 'that public order in which equality and good morals place all people in the same condition to exercise legislative powers usefully.' Citizens must join the nation by a solemn act of contract. The nation is not an aggregate of men, women and children, but a confraternity of faith. The rights of the citizen come only from the Social Contract. They also point out that equality of votes is illusory because of the inequality of assets, thus again necessitating the abolition of any form of private property.

He also advocated provisional revolutionary dictatorship.[18] This is because it is necessary to eliminate elements which distort the expression of the sovereignty of the people. This task of purification took precedence over the act of willing. What was required was war against the enemies of the people and re-educating the masses so that they could will freely (what they were expected to will by the revolutionary élite). This state would continue until all its enemies were overpowered and defeated and the Goal achieved.[19]

What did the Revolution amount to – other than the ultimate triumph of the bourgeoisie?[20] William Doyle says:

> An agreement about the principles contained in the Declaration of the Rights of Man and the Citizen. Despotism, aristocracy, privilege, feudalism, – all were gone. Sovereignty now resided in the Nation alone, a body of free and equal citizens bound only by the law, the expression of their general will as interpreted by their elected representatives. The end of political life was to conserve the natural and imprescriptible rights of man – liberty, property, security and resistance to oppression. Thought was free, expression was free, and the law was the same for everybody. ... Those who held the public office were accountable to the nation.[21]

Before 1789, the modern idea of state was only half-formulated if we define a state as an autonomous political unit recognising no sovereign power over itself outside itself. Certainly no Catholic state could have said that. It has been pointed out that the birth-year of the idea of the nation state is 1789.[22] In Germany, there were over 300 autonomous territories, but all were technically part of the Holy Roman Empire. Few states had formal written constitutions before this. The first was that dictated to the Swedish diet by Gustavus III in 1772 and the first to be adopted by agreement was the American Constitution in 1787. Before that, a 'constitution' was a collection of customs. After the French Revolution, there was a positive deluge of constitutions written or proposed. There were also egalitarian movements everywhere even though, as we know, the French Revolution ended in Napoleon as a dictator. Forces were irreversibly set in motion. It was the period, especially 1815-1840, of social revolution[23] and the rise of nationalism and romanticism.[24]

The period of 1848-1870's was a period of nationalism and nation-building based on a common history, culture, ethnic background and language.[25] Those who championed the nation-state also said that it must be 'progressive' (i.e. capable of an economy, military, etc.) This also coincided with the growth of liberal capitalism (under its various historical guises).

Having eliminated the absolute monarch as the focus of allegiance, the nation-state became the 'natural' unit of the modern, liberal bourgeois society. Civic religion or patriotism became the new legitimacy and source of loyalty.[26] The nation-state was the vehicle of the bourgeoisie who had control of the economy and used the slogans of 'nationalism' and 'democracy' to mobilize the support of the non-bourgeois. Liberalism was the economic flag of the new movement.[27] Liberalism was held to represent science, reason, history and progress.[28] The nineteenth century had seen a massive growth in population and a growing concentration of an industrial population. Such concentrations of non-bourgeois people had to be controlled, especially in view of the advance of universal male suffrage.[29] More sophisticated methods of social control were called for.

A major shift occurred in the nineteenth and early twentieth centuries. Bourgeois opinion had held that democracy and capitalism were incompatible,[30] but since the Cold War,[31] bourgeois ideologists have maintained that *only* capitalism is compatible with democracy. Capitalist control of production creates an internally competing, peacefully disunited ruling class. Of course, this means that those who ostensibly are the political rulers are not really the 'ruling' class at all because eventually they must be subject to the dominance of those who control the market and the currency.

Capital is divided into several parts – mercantile, banking, industrial, and agrarian (large and small). Outside of war, there is no unifying element in the system except for capital. The nation-state is thus the manifestation of the economic and political dynamic of the rise of capitalism.[32] The nation-state is freed from traditional restraints and loyalties.[33] The market replaced feudal ties.[34] Democracy makes everyone equal customers and in the modern global economy, the nation-states have become global customers of the banks. This is only possible by credit.

The bourgeois vision is based:

> ...on common assumptions, common beliefs, common forms of actions...They believed in capitalism, in competitive private enterprise, technology, science and reason. They believed in progress, in a certain amount of representative government, a certain amount of civil rights and liberties, so long as these were compatible with the rule of law and with the kind of order which kept the poor in their place. They believed in culture rather than religion... They believed in the career open

to enterprise and talent... it meant superiority.[35]

Such a vision is subject to manipulation of the worst kind by the unscrupulous if they are in control of the financial structures, particularly those on the *outside* of the clique who want in. War, a very expensive undertaking, but a very common one with a multiplicity of nation-states inspired by nationalism, allowed a small number of Jewish bankers to exert disproportionate influence.[36]

Ultimately the goal of such a system is to have all nation-states (customers) speaking a common language under an umbrella international organization which can regulate the global marketplace. The United Nations is being groomed for its future role as inter-national suzerain.

What hope has the authentic human being in such a scenario? It is the total reification of man. Unconsciousness rather than consciousness. Dumb silence instead of wisdom. Sub-human contentment instead of happiness. The ultimate end-result of the project of the Enlightenment, which was the deification of man,[37] is meaninglessness and the utter enslavement of man.

NOTES

1. *La volonté générale est toujours droite.*

2. Rousseau also rejects democracy: 'There has never been a real democracy, and there will never be. It is against the natural order for the many to govern and the few to be governed. It is unimaginable that the people should remain continually assembled to devote their time to public affairs... In fact, I can confidently lay down a principle that...the less numerous sooner or later acquire the greatest authority.' *The Social Contract*, III, iv, p. 55.

3. As we have seen, this was later developed by Hegel to the point where the state became an organic entity of individuals representing their highest ethical life. Indeed, as far as Hegel was concerned, it was the nation-state which counted and not the individual.

4. They looked with disdain at the English system as being 'irrational' and without a guiding principle and beset by factions.

5. Rousseau opened the door to revolution when one considered the

system to be illegitimate, and his ideas became the source of many distortions which had dire consequences in the elevation of the position of the majority, which ultimately led to a totalitarian vision.

6. However, the net effect of Rousseau's ideas was not classical republicanism or Spartan virtue, but incipient nihilism. Sensibility as a criterion also makes the world into an interpretation.

7. Whereas the English tended to think of the state as ensuring property rights.

8. From 1730 to 1780 in France was a time of terrible inflation, up to 62%. There was a credit flight in the 1770's and lots of bankruptcies. There was the John Law disaster. The same thing was happening in England and things were particularly bad for the poor:

'The more the 'wealth; increased – if we go by the figures for Treasury revenue…the greater also became the general poverty… more than 4000 persons in 1730 were simultaneously in prison for debt. Famine raged in the countryside, and in the towns the proletariat was submerged in poverty and squalor. Conditions were no better in France…

'The money in circulation tempted people into spending more than hitherto. Everybody was running into debt, creditors were pressing debtors, rents for homes went up, and higher rents were demanded by landlords from tenant farmers. The nobility at Court, the burghers in the towns, the higher clergy – none of them managed to live within their means now that money ran so easily through their fingers.' Ernst Samhaber, *Merchants Make History*, pp. 259-260.

9. This type of approach was criticised by Edmund Burke who made the distinction between the metaphor of the state as an organism, the product of long, complex growth and the state as a machine, which could be dismantled and reassembled, the mechanical image foisted by the Revolutionaries.

10. Thus society becomes a joint stock company.

11. Saint-Just, *'L'idée particulière que chacun se fait de sa liberté, selon son intérêt, produit l'esclavage de tous.'*

12. The Committee of Public Safety.

13. Force is further justified, *'Le gouvernement de la Révolution est le despotisme de la liberté contre la tyrannie.'*

14. One factor in the rise of the Jacobins was the collapse of the paper money, the *assignats*. There was a veritable flood of paper notes and terrible inflation. This led to speculation. The Paris banking-house of Boyd, Ker and Co. bought merchandise for *assignats* on credit and when payment was due, paid with the devalued notes, having made a huge profit. Also involved were Jope and Co. in Amsterdam, Harman, Hoare

and Co. in London and Parish and Co. in Hamburg.

15. Who gave his name to the failed Conspiracy of the Equals.

16. This is stressed so much that a person who is able to do the work of several is a 'social pest' and should be annihilated as a public danger. It is crime to give higher reward for talent.

17. The Grand National Economy.

18. Another approach was anarchism, whose first main exponent was William Godwin (1756-1836) who started from the premise that men are basically good and said that it is fundamentally wrong for members of society to cede their power to the state. They should decide matters among themselves in the absence of state power. 'Few things can be more absurd than to talk of having promised obedience to the laws. If the laws depend upon promises for their execution, why are they accompanied with sanctions? ... There is but one power to which I can yield a heart-felt obedience, the decision of my own understanding, the dictate of my own conscience.'

19. The New World Order?

20. As ever, there are economic factors behind great political upheavals. France had been running up a huge debt with its wars from 1733-1783, the interest running at 8 to 10%. The interest alone gobbled up more than half of the revenue. The debt continued to mount because there was an annual deficit of 112,000,000 and the taxes imposed by the government were resented.

21. William Doyle, *The Old European Order* 1660-1800, p. 330.

22. K. Renner, *Staat und Nation*, p. 89

23. In spite of the social upheaval, by 1848 the only political change was the division of the Kingdom of the Netherlands into Holland and Belgium and the emergence of a Greek state.

24. Also pushed on by the bleakness of the Industrial Revolution.

25. This was accompanied by a major advance in schools so that the 'national language' could become the written and spoken language of the people. Furthermore, mass media is impossible without a standard language.

26. There is much to be said for Kantorowicz's view that the state took over the *corpus mysticum* of the Church and hence took on a quasi-religious signification. (See Ernst Kantorowicz, *The King's Two Bodies* (1957))

27. Sometimes to maintain the support of the proletariat, it was necessary to adopt more inflammatory labels: 'Reform', 'Progressive', 'Republican', 'Radical.'

28. Thus the right-wing opposition were resisting 'the force of history'.

29. German Empire from 1867 to 1871, France from 1870 to 1875, Spain 1890, Switzerland 1874, Greece, 1864, Bulgaria, 18799, Norway,

1898.

30. So John Stuart Mill was an opponent of democracy, advocating multiple votes for bankers, merchants, etc.

31. In fact, this term was underway before as H.D. Lloyd points out in *Wealth Against Commonwealth* (1894): 'Institutions stand or fall by their philosophy, and the main doctrine of industry since Adam Smith has been the fallacy that the self-interest of the individual was a sufficient guide to the welfare of the individual and society.' (p. 330)

32. By capitalism, I mean a usury-based economy. In America, critics termed its effects: 'The Gospel of Wealth'.

33. This is what is at stake in the Dutch vs. Spain in the 16th and 17th centuries; the English Civil War and Restoration; the U.S. Declaration of Independence; the French Revolution; the 1830 August Revolution in Belgium; the unifications of Switzerland, Italy, Germany and Canada, Australia and New Zealand; the Meiji Restoration in Japan, the constitutional Eider state in Denmark, etc. It was the aim of mercantilism.

34. Democracy does not equal financial equality. In the great exponent of democracy, the U.S.A., by 1900 nine-tenths of the national wealth belonged to one-tenth of the population. This in a 'classless' society. Capitalist democracy is certainly more effective in this aspect than feudalism or any other system. The control which this entailed was recognised by H.D. Lloyd in *Wealth Against Commonwealth* (1894) 'monopoly cannot be content with controlling its own business. The same law has always driven the tyrant to control everything – government, art, literature, even private conversations.' 'In all ages wealth has found that it must rule all or nothing ... Hence we find it in America creeping higher every year into the seats of control.' (p. 234) Once economic power could buy political influence, the victory was all but complete.

35. E.J. Hobsbawm, *The Age of Capital 1848-1875*, pp. 245-6.

36. We frequently find that it is the Jewish bankers who fund wars, e.g. in the American Civil War, the Confederacy was banked by Lehman Brothers and the Union and U.S. government by a number of Jewish banks, especially Seligman & Co, who became the official fiscal agent for the U.S. government after the war. Yet Jewish-controlled banks were only 9% of the banks in the U.S.A. In Germany, banks like the Rothschilds and Warburgs were major war financiers, yet again Jewish banks were only 3.3 % of the banks. Israel was a pay-off for Jewish financial support in World War II.

37. In which sense the Enlightenment can be seen as a secularization of the Christian concept of incarnation. Or it can be seen as the result of the post-Socratics who ignored the injunctions of Homer and Pindar, 'Do not strive to be a god,' and sought divinity through their intellects.

The moderns flipped things around and sought to become divine through will.

Tyranny Dressed up as Democracy

Modern democracy provides freedom – freedom for the pursuit of one's own interest, but subject to the tyranny of the majority. This is the will of the majority – or more precisely as expressed by many, the tyranny of the majority.[1] In other words, if you do not agree with the herd as a whole, you are a wolf – and must be removed or silenced. Alexis de Tocqueville, writing *Democracy in America* back in 1835, observed this tendency in America:

> I know of no country in which there is so little true independence of mind and freedom of discussion as in America…In America, the majority raises very formidable barriers to the liberty of opinion: within these barriers an author may write whatever he pleases, but he will repent it if he ever step beyond them. Not that he is exposed to the terrors of an auto-da-fé, but he is tormented by the slights and persecutions of daily obloquy…Before he published his opinions he imagined that he held them in common with many others; but no sooner has he declared them openly than he is loudly censured by his overbearing opponents, while those who think like him, without having the courage to speak, abandon him in silence. …the body is left free, and the soul is enslaved.

And Tocqueville was not the only critic of American democracy. John Fenimore Cooper (1789-1851) saw, 'how the rule of the majority must tend towards a witness and malignant tyranny, anti-social in its motives and evil almost beyond endurance to its effects.' John C. Calhoun stated in 1850 in the Senate, 'what was once a constitutional federal republic is now converted, in reality, into one as absolute as that of the Autocrat of Russia, and as despotic in its tendency as any government that ever existed.'

How does this come about? Social control based on consent is the most powerful form of control because it **produces** behaviour. Control by simple coercion is weak because it only amounts to censorship.

Of course, social pressure does exist elsewhere in small communities, but the so-called democratic process gives this process a bogus legitimacy in spite of the well-known fact that elections tend to mal-select (a sort of Gresham's law, bad candidates drive out the good) and hence fewer and fewer people vote as they come to realise that their vote is worthless. Still 'the consent of the governed' has a sort of talismanic whiff of legitimacy about it. Even if it were not for the fact that extreme equality is subject to manipulation by the few, this is still not an effective method of achieving social justice, as H. Taine pointed out in 1875, 'Ten million ignorances do not make up one knowledge.'

There is another question here which John C. Calhoun, as a spokesman for a South which was becoming increasingly marginalised by the dominant capitalist North, pointed out – the inherent flaw in a system based on a numerical majority, and it is worth a quick look at his analysis. First, of all, he denied the whole concept of social contract and natural rights upon which democracy is founded, and pointed out that a state of nature where man's natural rights were unlimited, as described by the contract writers, has never existed, and is contrary to the actual natural state of man which is both social and political. He goes on to discuss the necessity of governance:

'...The powers which it is necessary for government to possess in order to repress violence and preserve order cannot execute themselves. They must be administered by men in whom, like others, the individual are stronger than the social feelings. And hence the powers vested in them to prevent injustice and oppression on the part of others will, if left unguarded, be by them converted into instruments to oppress the rest of the community. That by which this is prevented, by whatever name called, is what is meant by *constitution*, in its most comprehensive sense, when applied to government.' (*A Disquisition on Government*, p. 7)

The question, then, for him was: 'How can those who are invested with the powers of government be prevented from employing them as the means of aggrandizing themselves instead of using them to protect and preserve society?' The answer is not mass democracy: 'The right of suffrage, of itself, can do no more than give complete control to those who elect over the conduct of those they have elected. In doing this, it accomplishes all that it can possibility accomplish. This is its aim – and when this is attained, its end is fulfilled... but in doing so, it only changes the seat of authority without counteracting, in the least, the tendency of the government to oppression and abuse of its powers.' (p. 12)

Nor is a written constitution capable of preventing the slide. Calhoun draws attention to the fallacious assumption that a written constitution with suitable restrictions on the powers of government is enough in itself to counteract the tendency of the numerical majority to oppression and the abuse of power. The reason is that the elected majority has no need of the restrictions of the constitution, and hence they would take a liberal construction of it while minorities would take a strict construction. 'But of what possible avail could the strict construction of the minor party be, against the liberal interpretation of the major, when one would have all the powers of the government to carry its construction into effect and the other be deprived of all means of enforcing its construction?' (p.26) The end would necessarily be the subversion of the constitution. Ultimately, 'the government would be converted into one of unlimited powers.' His fears were justified, and at the end of the Civil War, 'The tyranny of unrestrained majorities was left to work its will in triumph.'[2]

Alexis de Tocqueville, whose remarkable work is as valid today as it was 150 years ago, remarked that as equality and the desire for it grow, so grows the power of the state and that equality isolates men and produces in them an inordinate desire for material things, the desire to get their 'fair share of the cake'. When you want everyone to be the same, to be 'equal' which they clearly are NOT (by birth, wealth, ability, intelligence) – then the state must impose what it deems to be equality (universal sheepdom) on them. You need commissions of racial, cultural, sexual, religious equality – all tuned into the state to ensure that all the sheep meet the ruling criteria.

This is NOT a natural form of equality, and certainly not a true political equality where everyone is accorded the same political rights – which nobody actually believes would be functional on a large scale. This concept of equality was unknown until modern times and only extreme Marxism, which has been described as extreme utilitarianism, would advocate it.

Indeed, Arendt describes this sort of equality of condition as one of the most 'uncertain ventures of modern mankind'. Political equality has been perverted to a social condition. It is an entirely unnatural form IMPOSED on people in order to subjugate them in a way hitherto unknown. Rather than demanding action from its members and giving them any real freedom, society now expects a certain type of behaviour, based on innumerable and often unspoken rules – designed to 'normalise' its members and make them behave in a certain way. If you differ from the imposed grid of equality, then you must be 'abnormal', perhaps even socially pathogenic. While this occurred in past social classes through custom, it is with the advent of mass society, that all social groups have been absorbed into the same mass unit. It has been homogenized and control has become total. As Hannah Arendt points out, 'behaviour' has replaced 'action'.

Ultimately this leads to rule by bureaucracy, by 'nobody', the invisible hand. It is now impossible to localise responsibility, to find the source of power – it certainly is not located in the floor show put on by the politicians. If tyranny is government not held to give an account of itself, rule by nobody is the most tyrannical of all. 'It's the system,' meaning you cannot find anyone responsible. You cannot locate the centre of power.

The most effective and insidious form of government control is to induce others to have the desires that you have – to control their thoughts and desires. As Tocqueville and John Stuart Mill after him pointed out, the majority controls individuals by a sort of censorious emotional blackmail which suppresses individuality, smothers spontaneity and human capacity. Mill, in particular, inspired by Tocqueville's practical observations, says:

When society itself is the tyrant – society collectively over the separate individuals who compose it ... it practices a social tyranny more formidable than many kinds of political oppression, since ... it leaves fewer means of escape, penetrating much more deeply into the details of life, and enslaving the soul itself.

Mill also pointed out the role and function of mass

education:[3]

> A general state education is a mere contrivance for moulding people to be exactly like one another; and as the mould in which it cast them is that which pleases the predominant powers in the government, … it establishes a despotism over the body. (*On Liberty* (1859))

Here arises the whole realm of thought control and indoctrination – at home via the fixed agenda of propaganda on the T.V., at school through the need to conform, at work, at play – all controlled.[4]

Only safety valves are allowed – not TRUE expression of dissent. The term 'freedom of expression' is a misnomer. Certain things are simply not permitted to be discussed. Critical discussion of the holocaust is off the agenda. Indeed, in Germany it is actually a crime to question the state-accepted version. The play *Perdition* is off the venue. Prof. Ernst Nolte is not allowed to address Wolfson College because his lecture might attract protest, 'and even if it did not, his presence could be painful to some college members.' So 'freedom of expression' only extends to proponents of the current world order, and those 'dissidents' whose criticism does not strike at the heart of the order.

This is not surprising in a 'democratical system'. Back in 1850, John C. Calhoun, pointed out that in a system based on numerical majority, freedom of the press is as useless as universal suffrage against the abuse of power:

> …What is called public opinion, instead of being the united opinion of the **whole** community, is usually nothing more than the opinion or voice of the strongest interest or combination of interests, and not infrequently of a small but energetic and active portion of the

whole… It is used by them as a means of controlling public opinion and of so molding it as to promote their peculiar interests and to aid in carrying on the warfare of party… It is as incompetent as suffrage itself to counteract the tendency to oppression and abuse of power. (*A Disquisition on Government*, p. 58)

Who controls the political agenda? If we posit Arendt's position that power only belongs to a group, or Michels' iron law of oligarchy – then who is the group in power if not the usurious banking élites who control the whole scenario from behind the scenes? The logic of mass communication demands a logic of control by élites, who then produce 'meanings'[5] and prefabricated motives for action. Political organization is nothing other than the mobilization of bias, the values and procedures which operate for the benefit of certain persons. The 'democratic choice' is really nothing more than selecting from a set of pre-determined choices representing different facets of the same paradigm – but who makes the choices in the first place? Without first addressing this question, it is difficult to assess the modern political structure in its true colours.

The decline in faith and break-up of spiritual unity, or a reckless leap of human hubris, has resulted in a hopeless dialectical search for what Rousseau would call a 'legitimate society' based on the 'general will'. All modern political thinkers would, I believe, posit (hopefully, wishfully, or wistfully) 'enlightened self-interest' as the source of man's motivation, and hence there is no incentive to accept a human-devised structure if it is detrimental to one's 'freedom' or self-interest. A Declaration of Human Rights only became necessary at the end of the eighteenth century when it was decided that man and not God's command is the source of law. It is, in fact, indicative of the fact that men no longer possessed their rights which had been ensured by social and religious forces. They may have been in abeyance under a tyrant, but they were still understood to exist. They only need to be articulated and codified when they are in real and permanent jeopardy.

Even positing that Rousseau's general will is anything more than a romantic interpretation, which according to him is the only thing for which you could give up your independence, I cannot see it anywhere in evidence. There is an illusion of the sovereignty of the people, reinforced by the politicians and media. The concept of 'general will' has been railroaded and used to justify the *status quo* in the outward form of the majority of the majority, which Rousseau rejected. In fact, as we have already said, what we have today is really the majority of the minority. In classical or any other terms, this is NOT democracy. It is oligarchy, but the real oligarchs have concealed themselves. It would be more apt to call it a usurocracy. Rousseau's famous opening sentence to the *Social Contract* is as true, or truer, today: 'Man was born free and everywhere he is in chains.' In fact, it is worse, because he thinks that he is free and does not even perceive the chains since he is too busy trying futilely to have a good time!

Looking beyond the slogans – why football and national ID cards, why the poll tax, why break up local authorities, local education authorities and centralize the lot? Why impose a Euro culture on everyone? To tighten the chains, to atomise social groupings, to make the sheep subject to the same shepherd – to uniformise, homogenise and control. If people become powerless individuals, each directly subject to the state, control is complete. THE INDIVIDUAL CAN NEVER ACHIEVE POWER ON HIS OWN. Power derives from the group acting in concert, not from an individual trying to exercise it. Even in Rousseau's terms, the social contract cannot come into force without an association of people with a common interest. Indeed, in his view, if there is exploitation and no common interest, then the social contract is broken and revolution – even anarchy – is justified.

The thinkers who are thought of as the formulators of the modern state would be shocked at man's degradation today, a degradation which Tocqueville foresaw when he describes the new despotism: 'The will of man is not shattered, but softened, bent and guided; men are seldom forced by it to act, but they are constantly restrained from acting. Such a power does not destroy, but it prevents existence; it does not tyrannize, but it compresses, enervates, extinguishes, and stupefies a people, till each nation is reduced to be nothing better than a flock of timid and industrious animals, of which the government is the shepherd.' (p. 580). Others have described it as 'the torpor of unanimity'.

The fact of the matter is that the 'democratic' experiment has come to an unsuccessful conclusion as far as human liberty is concerned. The only thing man is free to do is become a pawn in the game of Market Forces.

Property and ownership is not the be-all and end-all of human associations.[6] What concerns us is how people behave with one another and so, of course, property has its place in this. More important is defining the limits of behaviour and agreements between people. These may or may not involve property as the case may be. Man has forgotten his potentiality and the role that political organization can play in encouraging virtue, sunk as he is in a morass of doubt and alienation.

Now we can see that real democracy does not exist anywhere. There is no 'democracy' in the proper sense of the word, only the trappings of democracy. It is an illusion, a device to cover up what is in actuality an unseen oligarchical tyranny based on the augmentation of the wealth and power of a small élite. The benign, faceless despotism foreseen by Tocqueville is in fact the norm. It is clear that constitutions are useless – the existence of a constitution merely makes the people think that they are safe. Voting provides the illusion that they are participating in the determination of their future. Small wonder that only a minority continues the charade of voting. Indeed, the modern state itself is powerless, being in thrall to the banks. Their freedom of action is limited to the arena allowed by their creditors, and it is a morally bankrupt arena. John Dunn says:

> There simply is no plausible capitalist vision of a morally possible future for human beings even in the most flatly utilitarian of terms, each country for one and none for more than one – just as there can be no morally approbatory vision of the existing world order which is not based on a pronounced degree of moral astigmatism or myopia.[7]

So is there a natural form of political expression? If so, what is it?

The difference between the old and the modern is the difference between the God-given system wherein spiritual values are paramount and the man-devised system, which we find is ultimately based on property and ownership, in one way or another. Utilitarian ethics will not work. If we fail to take the divine into consideration, we will find ourselves the subject of tragedy. As Rosen says:

> From the very beginning, hermeneutics has been concerned with the communication between gods and mortals... . As a consequence, divine commands either found or dissolve communities. The interpretation of a divine command is necessarily a political act. The link between hermeneutics and politics can be broken only by anarchy or silence, in which case the recipients of divine revelations are transformed from citizens into hermits,

wandering in their respective private deserts, and at the mercy of the adjacent political authorities. (p.88)

This position is stunningly epitomized in the fate of Sophocles' Creon in *Antigone*, where we see that human law is justified to the extent that it expresses the God-given natural law. Creon's motives cannot be faulted – the common good, maintenance of stability and order, respect for laws. But he failed to take divine law and justice into account:

> The key to human happiness
> is to nurture wisdom in your heart,
> For man to attend to man's business
> And let the gods play their part:
> Above all, to stand in awe
> Of the eternal, unalterable law.
> The proud man may pretend
> In his arrogance to despise
> Everything but himself. In the end
> The gods will bring him to grief.

NOTES

1. This can be an 'elective despotism' as in the French revolutionary *gouvernement conventionnel*, or a single dominance of stronger elements or weaker, but stronger and more pernicious still is the social tyranny which controls behaviour.

2. Small wonder he is often maligned as a 'Southern secessionist' and advocate of slavery.

3. Of course, he himself advocated teaching utility as a religion!

4. An effective way of eliminating undesirable political or social groups is to portray them as 'folk-devils'. This is done through the 'myth-makers' (the mass media) who give the public their representation of the 'folk-devils'. Then the 'rule-enforcers', the formal agents of control, are authorized to deal with the 'devils' through criminalization – and then the devils are made to disappear.

5. Which one might well call meaningless 'signifiers' that in turn signify other meaningless signifiers. The metaphor of Rosen is apt: 'The

blind postmodern listens for the voice of Being; he hears nothing but the rustling of texts turning their own pages.' (p. 86) In postmodern society, everything signifies something else but nothing has meaning.

6. E.P. Thompson has a witty description about England joining the Common Market, written for the *Sunday Times* in 1975: 'It is about the belly. A market is about consumption. The Common Market is conceived of as a distended stomach: a large organ with various traps, digestive chambers and fiscal acids, assimilating a rich diet of consumer goods. It has no mind, no direction, no other identity: it is imagined as either digesting or in a replete, post-prandial state easily confused with benevolence or idealism. The image vegetates in the British middle-class subconscious. This Market has no head, eyes or moral senses. If you ask where it is going, or why, no one knows; they give an anticipatory post-prandial burp ('it will make us viable') and talk about bureaucratic procedures in Brussels. It has no historical itinerary. It lies in a chair, hands on its tummy, digesting a *pasta* of Fiats, a washing-up machine *meunière* and (burp!) that excellent *concorde thermidor* which may not have been as fresh as it should have been.'

7. John Dunn, *Western Political Theory in the Face of the Future*, pp. 81-82.

The Islamic Paradigm

The nature of governance in an Islamic context is a somewhat difficult question. Part of the difficulty lies in the fact that it has been a long time since Islam formed the foundation of governance,[1] and Muslims have tended to base themselves on Western political theories and then assiduously developed arguments, frequently naive and far-fetched, to 'Islamicize' them. It is for this reason that I will go into some details while describing the approach of Islam to governance.

THE MUSLIM POLITY

Even the question of what an *umma* is causes problems. Although the term is much in use today, the concept of the *umma* frequently remains somewhat nebulous and elusive. When it is translated as 'nation', it is inevitable that some of the connotations of the modern nation-state creep in, or if 'community' is used, it becomes a purely social concept, something like a commune. As the basic polity of Islam, it is worth first looking into what the *umma* is and the role it plays.

The concept of *umma* is seen both in the Qur'an and in what the Prophet Muhammad ﷺ said. It was an entirely new concept which superseded previous tribal and family allegiances. It wiped out the prevailing supremacy of kinship and tribal affiliations: *'You will not find any people who believe in Allah and the Last Day who are loving to anyone who opposes Allah and His Messenger, even if they were their fathers or their sons, or their brothers or their clan.'* (Qur'an 58:22) Acceptance of and allegiance to the *umma*, based on following Allah and

His Prophet, became one's primary allegiance. The *umma* is further delineated in the Qur'an when Allah says, *'You are the best umma brought forth to mankind – enjoining the correct and forbidding the incorrect and believing in Allah'* (3:110) and *'The believers, men and women, are protector-friends of each other, enjoining the correct and forbidding the incorrect.'* (9:71)

The Covenant of Madina stipulated that the Muslims 'Constitute one *umma*' and 'All believers shall rise as one man against whomsoever rebels or seeks to commit injustice, aggression, wrong action or spread mutual enmity between the believers, even though he be one of their sons. ... All believers are bonded together to the exclusion of other men.' Other groups are described as being other *ummas*. Mankind, then, is viewed as consisting of different *ummas*. So perhaps 'polity' might be a useful term in our context.

Contained within the Muslim concept of the *umma* is the idea that following the model of the Prophet ﷺ perfects character – i.e. virtue (*arete*), as the Greeks would have said. The Prophet ﷺ said, 'I was sent to perfect nobility of character.' The *umma* like the early *polis*, is a common project with shared values, concerned with all of man's life and providing a vehicle for the realisation of moral values and spiritual goals. It embraces all areas – social, religious, political, economic, spiritual, intellectual.

The *umma* also represents the mean, or the median way. *'Thus We appointed you a median umma.'* (2:143) It is also *'the best umma ever brought forth to men, commanding to the correct and forbidding the incorrect, and believing in Allah.'* (3:110) To maintain a balance in things is essential. Indeed, the root meaning of justice in Arabic, *'adl*, also carries a connotation of balance, of being the mean between excess and failing short.[2]

There are several common points between the Muslim *umma* – polity and the Greek *polis*:

1. Both are moral unities of peoples who have a common teleological position;[3]

2. Both seek self-transformation through ethical behaviour. In the *umma* on a social level, this is to 'command the correct and forbid the incorrect' (*al-amr bi'l-ma'ruf wa'n-nahy 'an al-munkar*) which was for the Greeks the capacity which distinguished man from beast;[4]

3. Obeying the laws of the polity is essential for its preservation. The *umma* is told, *'You who believe! Obey Allah and obey the Messenger and those of you with authority'* (4:59) – civil unrest[5] is seen as the worst of evils;

4. The people have a right to express themselves before decisions are taken – *isegoria* for the *polis* and *shura* or *mushawara* for the *umma*;

5. The median, or middle, way is the preferred way;

6. Both regard friendship as a political matter – the word for friends used in this context in the Qur'an, *awliya'*, also means protectors, guardians or managers and has a political connotation;

7. Stepping outside the *umma*, as in the case of the *polis*, results in becoming a barbarian. The Prophet ﷺ said, 'He who throws off obedience will meet God on the Day of Rising without any plea, and he who dies without having taken an oath of allegiance will die as a pagan [lit. the death of the *Jahiliyya*].'

The *umma* embraces anyone and everyone who accepts the basic tenets of the society (belief in the unity of God and the message of the Prophet ﷺ) and offers allegiance to it and those lands in which Muslim rule is established. Cultural heterogeneity, as long as it is not in conflict with the basic tents of the *umma*, is allowed. In other words, the political community is coterminous with the community of believers.

LEADERSHIP

So the polity in Islam is the *umma*.[6] Having defined our polity, then the question is how is it to be governed? There is agreement that it is a religious duty to have a leader – variously called the Imam or Khalifa.[7] As the jurist as-Subki said, 'According to the consensus of the Companions after the death of the Prophet 🕌, men should appoint an imam who will look after their interests. They gave this precedence over all other obligations and people have been abiding by this over the ages. Even if the appointed imam is not the most suitable, nevertheless the mere act of appointing him is sufficient to discharge the obligation.'[8]

Muslim law does not, however, concede absolute power to the ruler. Ultimate sovereignty belongs to Allah. The state does not create the law, but rather the state is created, maintained and defined by divine law.[9] The duty of the ruler is to defend and maintain and enforce the *Shari'a* – which is as binding on him as it is on his subjects. He cannot abrogate, amend, add to or even interpret the law. Thus he cannot exceed his authority and ask others to act contrary to the *Shari'a*.

When it comes to choosing the Khalifa, traditionally there were four ways that the Khalifa was chosen:

1. By the *bay'a* of the people of loosing and binding (*ahl al-hal wa'l-'aqd*) i.e. the *'ulama'* (people of knowledge), leaders and army commanders, as happened with the first Khalifa, Abu Bakr;

2. By the will and appointment of the preceding khalifa as happened with the second Khalifa, 'Umar ibn al-Khattab;

3. By a decision of the consultation (*shura*) of a certain group – as with 'Uthman and 'Ali, the third and fourth khalifas;

4. By the successful assumption of power of a man possessing the requisite qualities and qualifications to be khalifa (sometimes in conjunction with 1 or 2).

From the beginning, the Muslims (except for the Shi'a) were keen to keep the khalifate from becoming something hereditary.

As Muhammad 'Imarah says:

> There was an intention – in the beginning at least – to take it (*khilafa*) away from the family of the Prophet so that political authority did not become associated with heredity in order to ensure that none of the Prophet's family at any time could assume the Prophet's religious power because they inherited his political authority.[10]

Two areas are important in the legitimacy of the ruler or khalifa – *shura* (consultation) and the *ahl al-hall wa'l-'aqd*. *Shura* is based on the Qur'anic instructions: '*Consult with them about the matter*,' (3:159) and '*their business is mutual consultation between them*.' (42:38). It was practised by the Prophet who consulted his people on major decisions, and this aspect of regular consultation between ruler and ruled will be referred to later. As far as selecting a khalifa is concerned, it was used by 'Umar to determine his successor when he set up a council of six to decide who was to be the next khalifa. Iran claims to make use of *shura*, but in fact it is nothing more than a synonym for an American style consultative electoral system which has nothing whatsoever to do with the *shura* of the Muslims.

The *ahl al-hall wa'l-'aqd*, lit. the people who loose and bind, are those qualified to make such a decision. Originally the qualifications to be in this category were justice, the requisite knowledge to ascertain who possessed the prerequisite qualifications to be khalifa,[11] and reason and prudence, but it was later applied to all the élite and prominent people.[12] So it amounts to the elective body. As al-Laqqani says, 'This law [to appoint and instal an imam] is addressed to the whole community, as from the death of the Prophet ﷺ until the Day of Rising, but when the *ahl al-hall wa'l-'aqd* perform this task, it suffices for all.' (*al-Ithaf*)

When the khalifa has been chosen, *bay'a* takes place. It is an act of validation by which the ruler accepts the duties of office and receives the power to discharge them, and the subjects undertake to obey him. It is usually translated as 'allegiance' but this is somewhat unfortunate because it is an agreement undertaken by two parties, like the conclusion of a sale from which it is derived.[13] Each side has an expectation of the other. In essence, the khalifa makes an undertaking or covenant (*'ahd*) to act according to the *Shari'a*.

Hence the ruler has certain duties. He must respect and enforce the *Shari'a* and thus he must protect the interests of the *umma*, defend or expand the frontiers, carry out *jihad*, administer public property, dispense justice and maintain internal security.

The behaviour of the ruler vis-à-vis his subjects is a trust and a matter of grave concern for him in this world and the Next. The ruler is empowered to implement the *Shari'a* and all that entails, but he is nevertheless a custodian, and he expects to be corrected by the people of knowledge if he errs. When Abu Bakr was given the *bay'a* as Khalifa, he stood up and addressed people, saying:

> O people! I have been put in charge over you, but I am not the best of you. If I act well, then help me, and if I act badly, then put me right. Truthfulness is a trust and lying is treachery. The weak among you is

strong in my sight until I restore his right to him, Allah willing. The strong among you is weak in my sight until I take the right from him, Allah willing. People do not abandon *jihad* in the way of Allah but that Allah afflicts them with humiliation. Shamelessness does not spread in a people but that Allah envelops them in affliction. Obey me as long as I obey Allah and His Messenger. If I disobey Allah and His Messenger, you owe me no obedience. (*Sira* Ibn Hisham)

This clearly indicates the existence of a certain reciprocity in the relation between ruler and ruled. Abu Bakr's successor, 'Umar ibn al-Khattab was also concerned about overstepping his authority.

Salman said that 'Umar said to him, 'Am I a king or a khalifa?' Salman answered, 'If you have taxed the lands of the Muslims one dirham, or more or less, and applied it to unlawful purposes, then you are a king, not a khalifa.' And 'Umar wept. (At-Tabari, *Tarikh*, p. 2754)

So in this early vision of leadership, the khalifa has conditional rather than absolute authority as a despot would have. The word which Abu Bakr used when he took charge is from the root *waliya*, which refers to a guardian (*wali*) or heir or executor. He is someone who manages things for a person in their best interests – a custodian.

Abu Bakr called himself 'the khalifa (successor) of the Messenger of Allah'. Rather than onerously being called 'the khalifa of the khalifa of the Messenger of Allah,' 'Umar came to be called *amir* which comes from the term for the commander of an army.[14]

When we discuss things like authority and command, or even 'state' or 'leader',[15] in Islam, we run into problems because these are not terms intrinsic to Islam – they have been adopted from the West and employ Western concepts. Various words are employed for them and there has been a whole evolution of the terminology. This merits some discussion because of the nature of past leadership in many Islamic countries which is not in accordance with the Prophetic model.

Power and authority are not one and the same (as we have also seen in the West in *auctoritas* and *potestas*). Perhaps the closest to the two we can get in pre-Westernised Muslim sources is *hukm* and *'izza*. In Islam, *'All power ('izza) belongs to Allah'* (Qur'an 4:39; 10:65; 35:10) and so does *hukm* (6:57, 12:40; 12:67; 40:12, etc.) But Allah can also delegate *hukm* (authority) which involves jurisdiction, judgement and rule, to the Prophets, and hence to their successors. The Message is the source of the Prophet's authority, and implementation of the Message is the only validity for subsequent *hukm*. Certainly the Muslim form of leadership is not *Herrschaft*[16] as has been commonly misused for authority since Max Weber. The ruler is a guardian, a custodian and a shepherd, not a despot. Theophanes, the Greek chronicler of early Umayyad times, was surprised by the status of Mu'awiya, the first Umayyad khalifa, and refers to him as *protosymboulos* (first among equals).

The injunctions in the *hadith* literature regarding the behaviour of the Imam are quite severe, because he is answerable for the well-being of his subjects. First of all, governance is shepherdhood. The Prophet ﷺ clearly stated: 'An imam is a shepherd and is responsible for his flock.' (Ahmad, al-Bukhari and Muslim, at-Tirmidhi and Abu Dawud)

He also said, 'Any Amir who is appointed over the affairs of the Muslim and then does not strive for them and advise them well will not enter the Garden with them.'

And 'No slave is made shepherd over a flock by Allah and dies and is cheating his flock on the day he dies without Allah denying him the garden.'

APPLICATION

Shaykh Uthman ibn Fodio outlines the ten bases of justice which form the key to governance in his book, *Usul al-'Adl*:

1. The ruler must bear in mind that he has governance on trust. Abu Dharr asked the Prophet to put him in a position of command and he said, 'You are weak and this is a trust, which, on the Day of Rising, will bring shame and regret, save only to him who took it rightly and discharged the duties imposed on him.' Allah's laws must be applied without fear or favour, meticulously and untampered;

2. The ruler must have upright and courageous scholars to advise him and he must listen to their advice. The scholars have a duty to advise the ruler on what is best for ruler and ruled and not fear his displeasure. They are obliged to raise their voices against injustice or what is not correct. If the ruler fails to establish justice, then they must sever relations with the ruler;[17]

3. The ruler must ensure that all branches of his government also govern justly, because he is responsible to see that justice is established everywhere;

4. He must put himself in the position of his people when he introduces a policy. If he were to implement a policy detrimental to the people, that would constitute a misuse of his authority. It is said that the ruler should treat the old person as a father, the middle as a brother and the young as a son;

5. He must maintain an open door to the aggrieved and oppressed. His job is to establish justice and

prevent injustice, not simply to devote himself to personal acts of piety;

6. He must not allow himself to be dominated by arrogance or anger;

7. He should employ forgiveness and forbearance, and avoid harshness. Allah says, *'If you had been harsh and hard of heart they would have scattered from about you.'* (Qur'an 3:159) It is related in *hadith*, 'I heard the Messenger of Allah 🕌 say in this house of his, 'O Allah, anyone who is appointed over any of the affairs of my community and is hard on them, then be hard on him. Anyone who is appointed over any of the affairs of my community and is kind to them, then be kind to him;''

8. He should use resources so that everyone has his basic needs taken care of and not allow his appetites to dominate him. Shaykh 'Uthman recounts the story in which 'Umar ibn al-Khattab asked someone whether he had heard anything objectionable about him. He replied, 'I heard that you put two loaves on the tray for your meals and you have two shirts, one for the night and one for the day.' He asked if there was anything else and the man said no. 'Umar said, 'By Allah, both these things shall also cease;'[18]

9. He should remember the Day of Judgement when he will have to account for his stewardship. The Prophet 🕌 also said, 'Anyone whom Allah appoints over any of the affairs of the Muslims and who is then blind to their needs, friendship and poverty, Allah will be blind to his needs, friendship and poverty on the Day of Rising;'

10. He should follow and emulate the model of the Prophet ﷺ who is the perfect model in all things.

There are certain areas of governance (*wilaya*) which the ruler must attend to as well:

1. He must have a *wazir* who is well-disposed to the people and distinguished by his knowledge. The obligation is derived from the Qur'an as Shaykh 'Uthman points out in *Bayan wujub al-hijra*: 'As for the office of *wazir*, it is in conformity with the *Shari'a*; it centres on a man, trustworthy both in his religion and intelligence, who is to be consulted by the khalifa in all matters of his concern. In the Book of Allah, Musa is reported as saying, *'Appoint for me from my folk a wazir, Harun, my brother, Confirm my strength with him,'* (20:29-31) and a tradition of the Prophet ﷺ says, 'My *wazir*s from the people of heaven are Jibril and Mika'il, and my *wazir*s from the people of the earth are Abu Bakr and 'Umar."

The root of '*wazir*' is a helper, someone who helps someone else to bear a burden. The Amir consults the *wazir* on all matters of importance. He must also be someone who is kind-hearted and well-disposed to the people. In Sokoto, he attended the Khalifa's council in the morning when he was in Sokoto and he also had a final say in the khalifal election. He travelled around the domains of the khalifate constantly and if a case was evident, he was empowered to make decisions on the spot. If the matter was a difficult one, it was referred back to Sokoto. It was his duty to let the Khalifa know of any injustices or problems in the land. He was also in charge of the public treasury.[19]

2. He must have a *qadi* (judge) or *qadis* whose

judgement is independent of pressure from anyone, including the ruler. This is an appointment made on the basis of ability.[20]

3. He needs someone who is equitable to collect *kharaj* tax.[21]

Others have described the structure of governance, al-Mawardi in a particularly structuralist form, who also described the duties of the governors or local amirs, whose brief only extends to what they have been specifically appointed to by the Khalifa. 'Umar ibn al-Khattab mentions the conditions which he imposed on governors: not to ride mules, not to wear fine clothes, not to eat choice food, not to employ chamberlains and not to close the door against people's needs and welfare. He would say to the governor: 'I do not appoint you over men's persons and honour nor over their wealth; I only appoint you to lead them in prayer and settle their differences equitably.'

Under the Sokoto khalifate, the local Amir had a specific code to follow which was spelt out in detail in their letter of appointment. The letter addressed to Ya'qub, the Amir of Bauchi has seven instructions. The Amir is to:

1. be consistent and stand by what he says;

2. be zealous in maintaining the mosques;

3. be zealous in praying in them;

4. study the Qur'an and its teachings;

5. study *fiqh* and its teachings;

6. maintain the markets and prevent illegalities there; and

7. wage *jihad*.[22]

This was designed to ensure that the standards of Islam were carried from the centre into the provinces. Any complaints against amirs were sent to Sokoto and the people would appeal to a different Amir who would convey the complaint to Sokoto, or else the *wazir* would deal with it in his travels. Inter-amirate disputes would be forwarded to the Amir al-Mu'minin.

OBEDIENCE

The duty of the subjects is to obey. *'Obey Allah, obey the Messenger, and those in authority over you.'* (Qur'an 4:59) The Prophet ﷺ said, 'Whoever gives allegiance to an Imam, let him give it with the clasp of his hand and the core of his heart. Let him obey him if he can.'

Then the question of legitimacy arises in the case of usurpers and tyrants – the two forms of deviance from the proper role of the ruler. What are the limits of obedience?

In principle, a ruler who does not possess the qualifications for leadership or is not properly chosen, is a usurper – a point much used by the Shi'a. The Sunnis basically came to accept whoever was in power. However all schools agree that if the ruler becomes an unbeliever, his rule is illegitimate, or if he states that what is obligatory in the *Shari'a* is not obligatory or what is unlawful is lawful or tries to make people not pray or fast, then his rule is illegitimate, in which case the duty of obedience can become the duty to disobey.[23]

If the ruler does not rule justly, then he is a tyrant. What then?

There have been two approaches to this – one is the quietist school in which you obey whatever the circumstances because anarchy is worse. In fact some of the proponents of this line become rather Hobbesian in their approach[24] maintaining that the Sultanate is purely based on military power (*shawka* – brute force) and is accepted for the sake of peace. It amounts to the axiom: tyranny is better than anarchy.

The more radical and dissenting line[25] also has its classical exponents like Abu Bakr al-Baqillani, the tenth century *faqih* who maintained that the community can depose a leader if: he reverts to disbelief or stops praying and encourages others to stop praying, for tyranny and corruption, insanity, senility or if he is a prisoner of war for a long time. Al-Mawardi says that the ruler can only be deposed either by *qahr*, falling into enemy hands, or *hajr*, falling under the influence of one of his assistants who might act contrary to the *Shari'a* and justice. It is worth noting that all the four Imams and the bulk of Maliki *fuqaha'* endured hardship and imprisonment rather than submit to improper demands by the rulers – which does *not* mean that they preached revolt.

The fifteenth century North African scholar, 'Abd al-Karim al-Maghili at-Tilmansani, was quite revolutionary in the advice he gave about the overthrow of tyrannical oppressors. He says in his *Ajwiba*, 'It is not reprehensible to kill unjust miscreants and their helpers – even if they pray and pay *zakat* and perform pilgrimage.' This is after ascertaining whether such a course will be the lesser of two evils. According to 'Uthman dan Fodio, this would refer to those who use outward Islam to veil unbelief and make every attempt to suppress Islam and the Muslims.[26]

THE MODERN SITUATION

A major dilemma now arises in the modern situation where the status quo of Dar al-Islam has been smashed, the khalifate and traditional Muslim power structures abolished, and the Muslims partitioned, willy-nilly, into nation-states governed by forms derived from the Western tradition which, as we have seen, follows a rationalist approach to governance, and placed under democracy, socialism, and monarchy – Western style. So what is the response to this – are we in Makkan mode or Madinan mode or what?

A major problem lies in the fact that there has been a change of view in the purpose of the state – brought about by forced immersion in Western political principles. In *fiqh*, the principal function of government is to enable the individual Muslim to practise the *deen* and fulfill his obligations to Allah – which, of course, also entails certain societal obligations. This is, at the bottom line, the sole purpose of the state for which purpose alone it is established by Allah, for which purpose alone those in authority possess any authority over others. The worth of the state can be measured by how much this is achieved. Thus the state as an institution in its own right is a usurpation.[27] The state does not have any intrinsic authority on its own. Although Muhammad 'Abduh (1849 – 1905) advocated government as a 'civil' institution, even someone like E.I.J. Rosenthal recognises:

> By definition, then, a state whose criminal and private law is not based on the Shari'ah is not an Islamic state, even when Islam is the state religion and the personal status law is the Shari'ah-law, be it entirely traditional or modernised in varying degree, and whether this personal status law is administered by judges under religious or state authority. (*Islam in the Modern Nation State*, p. 89)

The Muslim 'state' by definition **cannot** enact laws, so the idea of modern nations adopting the *'Shari'a'* is a contradiction in terms.[28] The 'state' has no jurisdiction over the *Shari'a*.

Today frequently Islam has come to be viewed as a means to political power in a manner which is often an almost knee-jerk reaction of despair[29] to the situation in which Muslims find themselves. The majority of the modern reformists find themselves in this situation, which is not particularly surprising as the bulk of them have risen from the bourgeoisie or the Western-educated establishment.[30]

This can be seen in the Ikhwan al-Muslimin in Egypt, founded by Hassan al-Banna' and ideologically expressed through the writings of Sayyid Qutb and his followers. According to Qutb, 'the foremost duty of Islam in this world is to depose *Jahiliyyah* from the leadership of man, and to take leadership into its own hands and enforce the way of life which is its permanent feature.'[31] Muslim leaders who do not implement the *Shari'a* are illegitimate because they use *Jahiliyya* and as such should be removed.[32] They are reactionally seeking Islamicization of political institutions and enforcing rigid codes of Islam, which are in the end, a Western style vision. Politically speaking, they are seeking Islamification of political institutions – in the short term, a rigid interpretation of Islamic legal codes. They wish to remove one methodology and replace it with another methodology, which is ultimately derived from the same manner of thinking. One is the flip-side of the other. If they truly wished to do away with the Western statist form and methodology, they would be clamouring for all Muslims to withdraw from the U.N.

In what might be called the modernist quietist approach, there are attempts to reconcile Islam with, variously, nationalism, democracy and socialism, and probably now, market forces. This is really a dead-end because these are secular concepts for which there is no real Muslim alternative.[33] Traditionally there is no word for 'citizen'.[34] Man, as the viceregent of Allah (Qur'an 2:30) already has an elevated position, indeed, the highest possible position, while man, *homo*, in Latin is basically an entity without rights. The term traditionally used for the subjects is usually *ra'iyya*, or flock. There have been some fairly ingenious attempts to equate Islam with socialism or democracy. However,

Islam rejects the concept of popular sovereignty because sovereignty belongs to Allah,[35] and the polity in Islam is not one of **subjects** or **citizens**, but one of **believers**.

The major problem facing not only the Muslims, but all mankind, is that man has forgotten his position in the cosmos. Particularly since the Enlightenment, he has devoted his energies to seeking power and mastery – he has tried to become the Lord and forgotten who the Lord really is. By attempting to control everything by rational definition or sheer unrestrained will, he has turned everything and everyone into objects. By refusing any restraints on his god-like mastery of all, he has in fact become bestialised. This is inevitable. The Prophet ﷺ said, 'Two hungry wolves loose among sheep do not cause as much damage as that caused to a man's *deen* by his greed for money and reputation.'

The Prophet ﷺ, who is the highest model of human perfection, said that he was a 'grateful slave'. Modern man certainly is not. And if he is not the slave of God, he will be the slave of others. And today, as we have clearly seen in the political and economic situation, virtually everyone **is a** slave of others.

There is a lesson for us in what 'Isa says at the end of *Sura al-Ma'ida* (Table):

> 'I said to them nothing but what You ordered me to say:
> 'Worship Allah, my Lord and your Lord.'
> I was a witness against them as long as
> I remained among them.
> But when You took me to You,
> You were the Watcher over them.
> You are a witness of all things.
> If You punish them, they are Your slaves.
> If you forgive them, You are the Almighty, the All-Wise.'
> ...
> The kingdom of the heavens and the earth

and everything in them belongs to Allah.
He has power over everything.
(Qur'an 5: 119-120, 122)

NOTES

1. With the notable exception of the Sokoto caliphate, which will be discussed more in depth in the course of this chapter, and which established Dar al-Islam based on the model of the Prophet 🕮 for the first time in centuries.

2. The quality of temperance or self-restraint, *hilm*, is as much valued within the *umma* as *sophronsyne* was by the ancient Greeks.

3. The *telos* of the *umma*, of course, has another dimension. In the *umma*, the goal is in the Next World in which actions done in this world are rewarded or punished. For the post-Socratic Greeks, the goal is a virtuous life in this world, perhaps seeking the divine in man through philosophy, this, incidentally, forgetting the injunction of Homer, 'Do not hope to be equal to the gods in thinking.'

4. Furthermore, in Aristotle we find that lack of the virtues simply amounts to defects of character, while in the *umma*, although wrong actions are indeed defects, wrong actions are wrong because they are breaches of divinely revealed law. They are acts of rebellion against God who is the source of the Law.

5. *Fitna* in Arabic. The French Revolution was initially referred to as *fitna* in Arabic before the influence of modernism caused it to be changed to an *inqilab* (overthrow). *Fitna* is not quite apt given the fact that the French Revolution replaced revelation by universal suffrage as the source of authority.

6. Except in the case of the Hellenistic political philosophers like al-Farabi for whom it was the *madina*, the city, his word for *polis*. He defines the 'virtuous city' as the minimum unit for the attainment of human perfection. This then aggregates into the 'virtuous nation', and when there is submission to the Just Imam, to the 'virtuous world-state'. He follows Plato's categories, the top one being the *madinu fâdila*. Democracy is *madina jamâ'iyya*, timocracy *madina karâma*, tyranny *madina mutaghalliba*, oligarchy *madina nadhâla*. Shah Waliy Allah also uses *'madina'*.

7. This would be the overall leader of the entire *umma*.

8. Which is a *fard kifaya*, a collective duty.

9. It has been pointed out that if you wanted to find a Western term for the form of Islamic governance, it would be nomocracy, where the Law (Shari'a) is paramount.

10. *Al-Islam wa's-Sulta ad-Diniyya*, p. 15. 'Umar also excluded his son

from being considered for succession to the khalifate after him. Dynastic succession did not begin until the Umayyads, where it was most likely adopted as a means of avoiding civil war every time a khalifa was chosen – in fact, as the lesser of the two evils.

11. There are certain qualifications to be the Imam in classical tradition. He must be 1. a Muslim; 2. just; 3. male; 4. free; 5. adult; 6. of sound mind; 7. a *mujtahid* if possible, and if not, *muqallad*; 8. courageous; 9. possessing sound judgement; 10. able to execute decisions; 11. Qurayshi if possible.

12. In Sokoto the khalifa was elected from a *shura* of those in authority itself (i.e. the *wazir*, etc.) and the territorial leaders or amirs. The family of the khalifa were excluded from the election process.

13. *Ba ya 'a* is to barter, buy and sell, a transaction usually completed by a clasping of hands.

14. Other terms are possible and used later on in Muslim history. From 935, *Amir al-Umara'* (Amir of the Amirs) was used in Baghdad, and Shah Waliy Allah uses '*Imam al-A'imma*' (Imam of the Imams).

15. e.g. 'leader' could be *ra'is* or chief, which is pre-Islamic but uncommon, and used initially for heads of non-Muslim religious communities. Then it became an Ottoman admiral (*reis*) and is now used for a President. More apt is *zâ'im* (which is used for terms like *duce, führer, caudillo*), which was pejorative, with the stress on the pretence – used for the Old Man of the Mountain of the Assassins, the Zaydi Imam of Yemen or the Muwahhid leader. The Mamlukes used it as a military title, and in the nineteenth century it became the term for the modern leader.

16. Originally *Herrschaft* connoted seigniority and thereby domination and mastery. Hence it is a term whose concept derives from the Byzantine theocratic tradition (see above) and thus cannot be used in an Islamic sense – except perhaps in cases like that of the Umayyad 'Abd al-Malik (r. 685-705) who called himself '*Khalifat Allah*' in order to rival the Byzantine Emperor. It is not as Weber describes *Herrschaft*, 'Like the political institutions preceding it, the state is a relation of men dominating men, a relation supported by legitimate violence. If the state is to exist, the dominated must obey the authority (*Herrschaft*) claimed by the powers that be.' [Max Weber, *Essays in Sociology*, 1946] *Herrschaft* might legitimately be applied to Abbasid rule, but that was due to the influence of the imperial Sassanid legacy.

17. Earlier in Timbuktu, the scholars were considered to be the conscience of the people and never subservient to the rulers. The ruler would visit the Qadi and not the other way around.

When a ruler becomes arbitrary or capricious, acting on his own without due consultation of the people of knowledge, it is called *istibâd*, going it alone, a term which came to be used in the nineteenth and twentieth century for autocrats.

18. In Sokoto both the Khalifa and the *wazir* had *waqf* estates and were self-supporting, taking nothing at all from the Public Treasury.

19. Which consisted of *kharaj, jizya*, the fifth of booty and gifts (often sent at the times of *'ids*. *Zakat* was distributed locally. No tax except *zakat* was paid by the Muslims. There was also no *kharaj* paid in Sokoto proper because the land had been declared *waqf* for the benefit of the community.

20. This is an essential office and it provides a counterweight to arbitrary injustice on the part of the ruler if he comes into conflict with the Shari'a. It gives the people access to a means of rectifying wrongs so that they do not fester into discontent and, ultimately, rebellion.

21. Other minor offices are mentioned as well.

22. The amir is also forbidden by some from accepting gifts in this capacity. 'Attab ibn Usayd once said, 'By Allah, the only thing I gained from the work the Messenger of Allah ﷺ charged me with, was two garments which I gave to my client, Kaysan.'

23. Which must, of course, bring into question virtually all modern political leaders.

24. e.g. Ibn Jama'a (d. 1332), al-Mawardi (d. 1058) and al-Ghazali (d. 1111). As al-Ghazali said, 'The concessions which we hereby make are not voluntary, but necessity may render lawful even that which is unlawful ... Which is better, to declare that the qadis are revoked, all authorizations invalid, marriages cannot be legally contracted and all acts of government everywhere are null and void ... or to recognise that the imamate exists?

25. Which has modernist revolutionary manifestations, most of which would view the ruler as 'Pharaoh' and follow the Qur'anic injunction of disobedience to an unjust ruler. (26:151-152) *'Do not follow the command of those who are extravagant, who cause corruption in the land and do not put things right.'*

26. Ibraheem Sulaiman, in his excellent book, *A Revolution in History*, describes this category in reference to the situation in 'Uthman dan Fodio's time as when: 'Secular laws substituted for the Sharia, pagan customs and behaviour replaced Islamic social morality; oppressive taxation, usurpation and the confiscation of property replaced the Islamic system of taxation and fiscal policies; and Islamic inheritance laws were abandoned in favour of pagan whims.' (p. 123)

27. This, of course, raises the whole question of Muslim states being members of the United Nations. The U.N. Charter states (Art 21.3) 'The will of the people shall be the basis of the authority of government,' i.e. it does not accept divine authority. Then there is the whole problem of

the divergence of the Articles of the U.N. from Islamic principles, i.e. Article 4 prohibits slavery, Article 5 would outlaw *hudud* punishments; Articles 7,8 and 10 would prevent dhimmi status of non-Muslims, Article 16 would affect Muslim laws of marriage and Article 18 allows apostasy.

28. For all pious proclamations to the contrary, the discussion of power by Muslim activists is usually a very secularized and Westernized one couched in 'Islamic' language.

29. Part of the problem is that Muslims seem to be unaware that they too have been infected by the disease of 'Enlightened' rationality and its concomitant reification of everything. The result of despair – to which Enlightened thinking inevitably leads – is what could be called political decadence, one aspect of which resorts to elaborate methodology and codification of the Shari'a in a manner totally disconnected from natural life. Another symptom of decadence is the alacrity with which the cry of *bid'a* and *takfir* is raised, which is actually *ressentiment*. One of the amazing things about the life and writings of 'Uthman dan Fodio is the total absence of any *ressentiment* or political decadence.

30. Not surprising given the truism that along with the emergence of any 'democratic' system is the rise of an economic structure which in turn gives rise to an autonomous bourgeoisie.

31. *Milestones*, p. 245.

32. The rhetoric often smacks of Kharijism, particularly in its offshoot, *Takfir wa Hijra* where Shukri Mustafa says in his testimony before a military tribunal in 1977, 'Not everyone who claims to be a Muslim is one. Only those who accept and live by the tenets of the Jama'at al-Muslimin are good Muslims. Others are infidels.' Clearly they also envisage a contractual theory of government. This was explicit in the case of Hassan al-Banna' who refers to the ruler as a person responsible to his *umma* who must follow its opinion. There is clearly a democratic shift here.

33. One writer describes an Egyptian scholar as saying, 'While the cryto-socialists [in the Government and the intelligentsia] strive to vindicate socialism through Islam, the shaykhs are trying to prove Islam through socialism.' Hamid Enayat, *Modern Islamic Political Thought*.

34. Today new words have been invented for it: *muwâtin* in Arabic, *shahr-vand* in Persian and *vatandàs* in Turkish. Similarly words have been invented for 'secular' – *ladini* (non-religious) in Turkish and then *lâyik* from the French, and in Arabic *'alâmânî* (worldly) was borrowed from the Christian Arabs.

35. Qur'an 18:44: *'Sovereignty (walaya) belongs to Allah, the Real.'*

www.ingramcontent.com/pod-product-compliance
Lightning Source LLC
Chambersburg PA
CBHW030024290326
41934CB00005B/478